PSI SUCCESSFUL BUSINESS LIBRARY

MARKETING MASTERY
YOUR SEVEN STEP GUIDE TO SUCCESS

Harriet Stephenson and Dorothy Otterson

Edited by Erin H. Wait

OASIS PRESS
BOOKS & SOFTWARE

The Oasis Press® / PSI Research

Grants Pass, Oregon

Published by The Oasis Press

Marketing Mastery: Your Seven Step Guide to Success, revised and updated
© 1995 by Harriet Stephenson and Dorothy Otterson

Originally published as *Marketing Your Products and Services Successfully*
© 1986 by Harriet Stephenson and Dorothy Otterson

This publication is designed to provide accurate and authoritative information
in regard to the subject matter covered. It is sold with the understanding that
the publisher is not engaged in rendering legal, accounting, or other professional service. If legal advice or other expert assistance is required, the services of a competent professional person should be sought.
> — *from a declaration of principles jointly adopted by a committee of
> the American Bar Association and a committee of publishers.*

Editor: Erin H. Wait
Format and Typographic Designer: Erin H. Wait
Book Design Consultant: Constance C. Dickinson
Assistant Editors: Vickie Reierson and Linda Pinkham
Cover Designer: Arthur Wait

Please direct any comments, questions, or suggestions regarding this book to
The Oasis Press®/PSI Research:

Editorial Department
300 North Valley Drive
Grants Pass, OR 97526
(503) 479-9464
(800) 228-2275

The Oasis Press® is a Registered Trademark of Publishing Services, Inc.,
an Oregon corporation doing business as PSI Research.

Library of Congress Cataloging-in-Publication Data
Stephenson, Harriet.
    Marketing mastery : your seven step guide to success / Harriet
Stephenson and Dorothy Otterson ; edited by Erin H. Wait.
       p.   cm. -- (PSI successful business library)
    Rev. ed. of Marketing your products and services successfully.
    Includes index.
    ISBN 1-55571-357-2 (pbk.) : $19.95. -- ISBN 1-55571-358-0 (binder)
: $39.95
    1. Marketing--United States--Management--Handbooks, manuals, etc.
2. Small business--United States--Management--Handbooks, manuals,
etc.   I. Otterson, Dorothy. II. Wait, Erin H. III. Stephenson,
Harriet. Marketing your products and services successfully.
IV. Title. V. Series.
HF5415.13.S873 1995
658.8--dc20
                                        94-47632

Printed in the United States of America
Second Edition 10 9 8 7 6 5 4 3 2 1 0

 Printed on recycled paper when available.

Table of Contents

Step 5 – Create Customer Awareness

Step 6 – Transfer Ownership

Step 7 – Follow Up and Obtain Feedback

Conclusion – Design Your Marketing Campaign

Charts, Tables, and Samples in this Book

Worksheets in this Book

About the Authors

Harriet Stephenson

Harriet Stephenson is the founder and director of The Entrepreneurship Center at Seattle University where, as Professor of Management, she teaches entrepreneurship and small business management and runs the Small Business Institute Program. She has served on several boards of directors and advisory boards. She has consulted on entrepreneurship curriculum and program evaluation nationally and internationally. Dr. Stephenson has authored or co-authored more than 50 refereed articles, books, and other publications, including items on the marketing process, microenterprise, and ethics for small business. She has owned her own businesses and has consulted with many profit and not-for-profit businesses and organizations. Dr. Stephenson received her B.A., M.A., and Ph.D. in business from the University of Washington.

Dorothy Otterson

Dorothy Otterson is a marketing and management consultant who works with small business owners, professionals, and educational resource clientele to effectively develop their organizations through goals identification, marketing plans, tools-for-change management, project facilitation, and educational training and development. Ms. Otterson offers workshops and personal effectiveness training through her own home-based business, Otterson Management Associates in Marin County, California. She currently balances her time managing various microbusiness projects, developing and teaching courses, and focusing clients on their own goals and how to achieve them, with an emphasis on healthy growth management. She also works with not-for-profit organizations to develop their organizational effectiveness and maximize their available energy and resources. Ms. Otterson received her B.A. in marketing and MBA in organizational development from the University of Washington.

Preface

Small business is the backbone of America. Of the approximately 25 million businesses in existence in the United States, 97% can be classified as small. However, many businesses with high-quality products or services and good intentions do not succeed — due mainly to insufficient marketing skills.

Successful marketing is not the reserve of business-school trained experts. Anyone can master the marketing process. Simply consider how you can capitalize, at every opportunity, the customers' feelings of satisfaction with your product and your business. Your goal is to find customer needs and fill them — at a profit. To profitably find and fill customer needs, you must acquire core groups of customers that are satisfied-plus — customers who will tell their friends, family, co-workers, or supervisors how pleased they are with the product or service they purchased. Satisfied-plus customers help a business maintain a competitive edge, flourish, and grow.

You will learn in this book how to achieve marketing mastery using an interactive planner that leads you through seven key steps in the marketing process. By using the guidelines, reading the examples, and filling in the worksheets, you will be able to design a successful, personalized, and practical marketing plan — a marketing plan that leads you to satisfied-plus customers and to new customers.

Satisfied-plus customers can motivate your employees and managers by giving direct feedback that their work is valued and worthwhile. Satisfied-plus customers can also generate new leads and ideas for new products and services. You will not only have a strong customer base, but you will also have a motivated team of employees. All parts of your organization need to be responsible and knowledgeable about the marketing process to make your marketing efforts most effective.

This interactive workbook will teach you the techniques and strategies of successful marketers so that you can:

- Identify the unique characteristics of your product or service;
- Identify your target market segments to carve out your niche;

- Be aware of various business trends that can move your business into the twenty-first century;
- Determine an appropriate price for your product or service;
- Determine the most effective business location and ways to make your product accessible to your customers;
- Select the most cost-effective advertising media and sales promotions;
- Establish a workable marketing budget;
- Examine options to expand your market nationally, or even globally, as you grow; and
- Deliver customer satisfaction-plus.

Each chapter contains information that will take you one step closer to marketing mastery. The techniques in this workbook will give you the competitive edge you need to be an effective entrepreneur, today and in the future. Mastering all seven steps will enable you and your employees to grow with your business and constantly improve your marketing strategy and customer satisfaction over time.

We are concerned that you, our customers, are satisfied-plus. Please give us feedback through the publisher, or e-mail us at harriet@seattleu.edu or DOtterson@aol.com. What works? What do you want to see more of? What doesn't work? Did you find something you would like to tell others about?

Good luck! May your enthusiasm, perseverance, and a sharp marketing strategy pay off!

Harriet Stephenson
Dorothy Otterson
February 1995

How to Use this Book

The focus of this book is a seven step marketing process. Many people who start a business or have an idea for a new product fail to consider all the different levels of marketing. None of the most successful businesses, such as Microsoft, Federal Express, and McDonald's, would have succeeded simply with a good idea or a good product. Each of these businesses addressed the fundamentals of marketing — research, pricing, location, distribution, packaging, advertising, sales, delivery, and follow up. Moreover, none of these businesses considered these marketing fundamentals just once. They have continually reassessed the direction of their marketing efforts.

The strongest message in this book is that you should use it as an ongoing, interactive process that responds and conforms to your business' needs over the months and years ahead.

Organization

Marketing Mastery: Your Seven Step Guide to Success is divided into eight sections. The first seven sections represent each of the seven steps in the marketing process. The final section, the Conclusion, goes into some detail about how to personalize the methods and strategies you have learned to write your own marketing plan.

Worksheets

Marketing Mastery contains 31 worksheets that help you apply the methods and concepts you learn in each chapter to your particular business. The various worksheets will help you:

- Define your product or service;
- Write a customer profile;
- Write radio ad copy;
- Write a press release;

- Develop a marketing budget;
- Determine a pricing strategy; and
- Assess the cost and effectiveness of various advertising media.

In many cases, you will want to photocopy the worksheet before you fill it out because, as you go through the marketing process again and again in the future, your answers to many of the worksheet questions will change. The marketing process is ongoing, requiring you to constantly reassess and reevaluate your earlier assumptions about your product, your business, and your customers. Having extra copies of some worksheets on hand will help you with this process.

Three chapters contain an additional feature to complement the many worksheets. In two of the market research chapters, chapters 5 and 6, and one of the media selection chapters, Chapter 14, you will find interactive question boxes, like the one shown below, in which you can note any thoughts you have in response to the text, or answer specific questions about what you have read. You can then apply these answers to the appropriate worksheets. Chapters 5, 6, and 14 use these interactive question boxes because they compare and contrast specific types of market research and advertising sources.

Interactive Question Boxes

How will you use this seven step marketing guide to assure your business' success now and in the future?

_____

_____

_____

Other Helpful Resources

Several flow charts and tables are included to illustrate important concepts, such as the marketing process, current business trends, product profiles, and channels of distribution. You will also find sample questionnaires, surveys, and a press release from which you can learn how other businesses use the tools of the marketing process.

Finally, the authors have included several examples of businesses that use the seven step marketing process. From these examples you can witness how businesses use the steps of the marketing process to their benefit, and how businesses who fail to follow the marketing process suffer.

⇨ The example of the Evergreen Indoor Plant Nursery will take you through each of the seven steps, as Paul and Ellen, the owners, define their product, research their target market, set their price, develop product accessibility, purchase time on various advertising media, and design methods for initiating sales, delivering the product, and performing customer follow up. You will get to know the business as the owners struggle with the same marketing decisions you will face as you build your business using the techniques described in this seven step guide. The story of Evergreen's seven step marketing process will be set aside in text, as shown here.

This book gives you the conceptual knowledge necessary to carry you through the trials and errors of business and to refine the marketing methods that work best for you. The worksheets are flexible and interactive, designed to adapt to your particular marketing needs and serve as the building blocks for a comprehensive marketing plan. If you follow the suggestions and use the techniques presented here — constantly revising and updating your worksheet answers — you will build an effective blueprint for business success.

A Note from The Oasis Press

For the convenience of readers who may want to pursue a subject in more depth, The Oasis Press, the publisher of *Marketing Mastery*, has referenced appropriate titles from its Successful Business Library throughout the text. To order one of these suggested titles, refer to the Related Resources at the back of the book.

Step 1 – Define Your Product or Service

1 | The Marketing Process

Marketing is a continual, ongoing process. Before you can begin marketing your product or service, you need an overview of how the entire marketing process works. Many different factors play a role in how you develop and implement your marketing plan. To develop and grow your business, you constantly need to reevaluate your marketing plan to take into account changes in your business, your product, your customer base, and the business environment in general. If you evaluate your marketing campaign carefully, it can be sensitive to current business trends and can give you an advantage over your competition.

Your business will benefit in several ways if you develop a comprehensive marketing strategy. A well-planned marketing process enables you to effectively influence sales and business growth. In addition, most banks and lending agencies require that your business plan contain a synopsis of your marketing process. A successful marketing process motivates your employees to be responsive to customers and knowledgeable about your products. By reading this seven step interactive marketing guide, and applying these steps to your particular product or service, you will have the framework to develop an initial marketing campaign and a successful marketing strategy.

The flow chart on page 2 illustrates the seven steps of the marketing process and how they relate to each other. Each of these seven steps, described briefly on the next several pages, is an essential ingredient in the marketing process. At each step, your goal is to acquire satisfied-plus customers, customers who are so satisfied with your product or service that they will do all their repeat buying with you and tell their friends, family, neighbors, and co-workers to buy your product or service.

Step 1 – Define Your Product or Service

Think about your product. What are people buying from you? Your customers can see or describe a good or service. You can physically show or

The Marketing Process Flow Chart

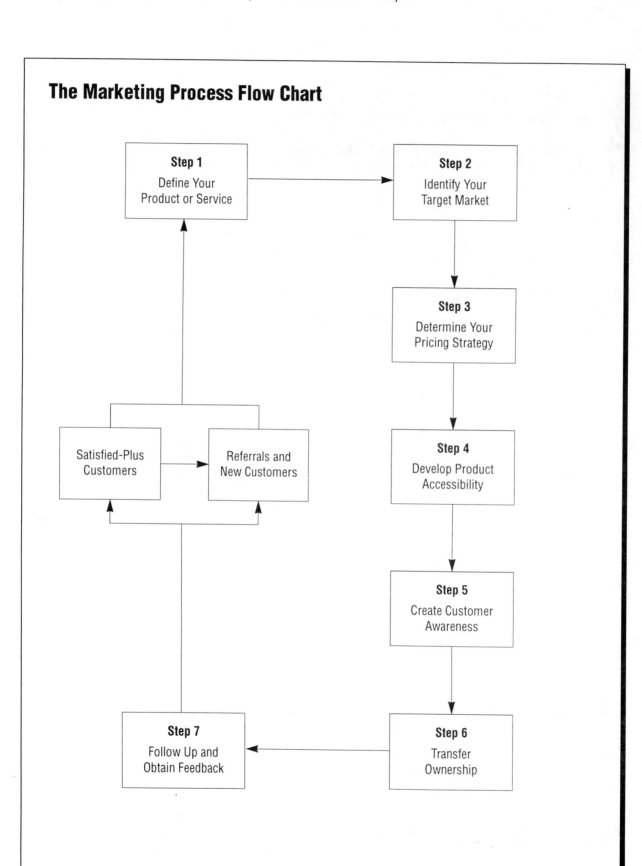

display the product you have for sale. However, these physical identifiers are not necessarily what your customers are buying. You need to define your product at another level — according to customer needs and expectations.

What does your customer want from the product? If you don't know what your customers expect when they buy your product, you won't know how to price it or tell potential customers about it. Do your customers view the product as a gourmet or luxury item? Do they think it is a necessity or a staple product? Chapter 3 discusses in more detail how you can define your product or service on several levels and according to various customer expectations, and how to write a product profile.

Once you have defined your product and how it meets customer needs on different levels, you will have completed the first step in constructing your marketing process.

Step 2 – Identify Your Target Market

Who is buying your product? Who do you think will buy it? What is the composition of your target market in terms of age, income level, education level, geographical location, marital status, interests, hobbies, or occupation? What do potential customers want from your product? What are they willing to pay for it? Is price particularly an issue? What feature of your product will satisfy potential customers? All of these questions need to be part of your market research.

Not everyone is a potential customer. You need to know who comprises your core customer base, the 20% of your customers who will account for 80% of your business. Identify them by finding out as much about them as possible. Chapters 4–6 will lead you through this step in more detail.

Step 3 – Determine Your Pricing Strategy

Once you know what your product or service is and who your likely target customers are, you need to develop a pricing strategy that attracts those customers, yet allows you to remain competitive and make a profit for your efforts. Pricing is an important step in your marketing process and can actually be considered part of what you are offering your customers. Price affects the perception in the buyer's mind of the total image he or she is paying for. Does your price suggest high quality and prestige or rock bottom value? What is your intention and how does your pricing strategy communicate that intention to your targeted customers?

The best pricing strategy is one that allows you to attract enough customers to prosper over the long run by covering costs and making a profit. Step 3 considers various pricing formats you can use depending on whether you are a wholesaler, retailer, manufacturer, or service provider. Some products and services are very sensitive to price changes. However, you can also use other factors, such as quality, convenience, and prestige, to differentiate your products and services. Chapters 7–9 cover both the concrete and the subjective aspects to pricing.

Step 4 – Develop Product Accessibility

Developing product accessibility is the fourth step in your marketing process. This step includes determining your business location, channels of distribution, and packaging. The image you portray to potential customers is affected by whether they are attracted to your business location, can find your product or service easily in the quantities they desire, and are aware of how your products and services are distributed. Deciding how to package your products and services — your logo, packaging colors and words, business work environment or storefront — is all part of how your customers perceive the total package you are providing and whether it is readily accessible to them.

If customers have to go too far out of their way to find your retail or service location, or to find the wholesalers or retailers who sell your product, they will be more likely to buy from your competitors. If your packaging design does not communicate the contents well or only allows customers to buy in bulk, your customers may be less likely to buy your product. Because sales are the goal of marketing, you must take these various factors into account as a vital step in your marketing process. Chapters 10–12 discuss the ways in which you can assure product accessibility.

Step 5 – Create Customer Awareness

Once you determine your niche — who is buying from you and why — and distinguish your product or service from others on the market, you can communicate to your target market that you have what they want at a price they are willing to pay. You can communicate where and how they can get the product and the particular benefits they can expect to receive by purchasing it.

The means by which you create awareness of your product among your customers must be appropriate to your target market. When you perform Steps 1–4 of the marketing process accurately and thoroughly, you will be prepared to choose the best advertising media for your target market. The better you know your customer or customer-to-be, the better you will be able to focus your marketing efforts to communicate the right message, using the best media and methods to sell your product.

Step 6 – Transfer Ownership

The sixth step in the marketing process is to transfer ownership — to take the order, close the sale, and deliver the product. How easy or difficult is it for the customer to actually buy the product, to write a check, hand over cash, or charge the purchase on a credit card? Is an order form immediately available? What does the customer experience during this stage — pleasure or frustration? If your product is expensive, do customers experience buyer regret, or think, "Maybe I shouldn't have spent so much?" You need to consider this phase of contact between customers and your product, how smoothly it will go, and whether it will cause your customer to come back for more or recommend your business and your product to others.

You also need to consider the quality of the interaction between customers and your sales staff or other representatives of your business. What can you or your staff do to make your customer's experience positive? Some customers may return to buy a product from you, even if they know where to get the same item elsewhere for less money, if their experience making the purchase is positive and trouble-free. Well-trained customer service representatives and sales staff are crucial to this step in the marketing process.

When your product is physically received by the customer or your service is provided, what do you do to reassure customers that they have made the right decision to buy from you? How do you instill confidence that the quality of the product or service is what the customer hoped for and more? A quality physical presentation of the product at the time of delivery — its packaging, the shopping bag, your delivery van — can enhance the customer's perception that the product itself is of high quality. You want the customer to be reassured that the product works or does what it is supposed to. If the product arrives with the correct parts, in the right color, and at the time promised, the customer will believe that he or she is closer to being able to use or experience the product as anticipated.

Step 7 – Follow Up and Obtain Feedback

Making certain the customer is able to get what he or she expects from the product over time requires follow-up customer service after your customer takes home and begins to use your product. Does the piano hold its tune? Does the computer have the kind of speed or memory the customer wanted? Does the mower start as well on the second or third time as it did the first? Is it working like the customer expected?

Try to get feedback from your customers a few weeks or months after they begin to use your product, perhaps with a follow-up phone call, brief on-site visit, or direct mail questionnaire. Your customers need to hear again how important they are to you and that you are concerned about providing a quality product. Is the product's quality what your customers want and expect? What else can you do to ensure the product's quality or your customers' enjoyment of it. What can you do if you find disgruntled customers weeks or months after they purchased the product? Will you give a refund? Will you replace the item or provide the service again and get it right in the eyes of the customers? What other products would the customers like? Would they like any changes in the products?

The feedback period is also a good time to get referrals. Should anyone else know about the product? Satisfied customers don't mind letting their friends and colleagues share in good quality. When your marketing process works, you will have customers who are satisfied-plus — repeat customers and potential new customers acquired through word-of-mouth advertising and follow-up referrals. Satisfied-plus customers are motivated to tell others about your product and eager to see you succeed. They will give you information to help you keep them as repeat customers, and they will often make suggestions for new products you should offer to attract new customers.

To ensure that you constantly cultivate your core satisfied-plus customers, you need to perform follow up as the seventh step in your marketing process. Are your customers coming back? Are they telling their friends about you? As you analyze these questions, begin again at the initial step, to define your product or service. Are the customers you originally designed the product for still buying it? Do your customers use your product in the way you envisioned they would? Redefine your target market, redesign your pricing strategy, reassess your product's accessibility, reevaluate your advertising campaign, readjust your transfer of ownership methods, determine if the product or service needs modifying or has additional marketing possibilities, and finally, follow up.

Marketing Process Summary

Only by closing the loop, by doing follow up and starting over at the beginning, will your marketing plan be an effective process. Only as an ever-changing process can your marketing plan take into account changes in business trends and truly become a marketing strategy.

However, the economy and the business world are not immune to major business trends. Knowing these trends can give you a tremendous sales advantage over your competition, but failing to keep abreast of business trends could lead to your business' demise. Chapter 2 examines some of the most important business trends that can influence and enhance your marketing effectiveness.

2 | Current Business Trends

While your business may not be as susceptible to outside forces, such as political or social movements, as other businesses, you should prepare for every contingency, particularly those that can enhance your business' competitive edge. You need to know how your business, your product, and your customers compare to those of your competitors. You need to know what you can offer customers that your competitors can't — your competitive advantage. One way you can gain a competitive advantage is to keep abreast of trends in the marketplace.

The economy can change so rapidly that you need to be aware of the latest trends and prepare for them. To prolong your marketing process' probability of success, you need to pay attention to external factors that exert a strong influence on the marketing process. Seven of these current business trends, or competitive edge trends, are described below. As you work through the manual and do your research, note which of these trends affect your competitive edge.

Home-Based Businesses

More than 40 million home-based businesses are now established in the United States. Some home-based businesses probably do no more than provide jobs and income for their owners. Others grow to become national, or even international organizations. With successful marketing, your business can grow to be as large as you want or need it to become. Beginning as a home-based business to keep operating costs low is one way to assure that it will.

Several million home-based businesses are part of an informal or underground economy, operated on a cash-only basis and not as officially licensed or taxed businesses. Much of what is now called microentrepreneurial activity, business activity involving only one to five people, is operated out of the home. For example, a beautician, writer, or piano teacher may start his or her business out of an extra room in the house.

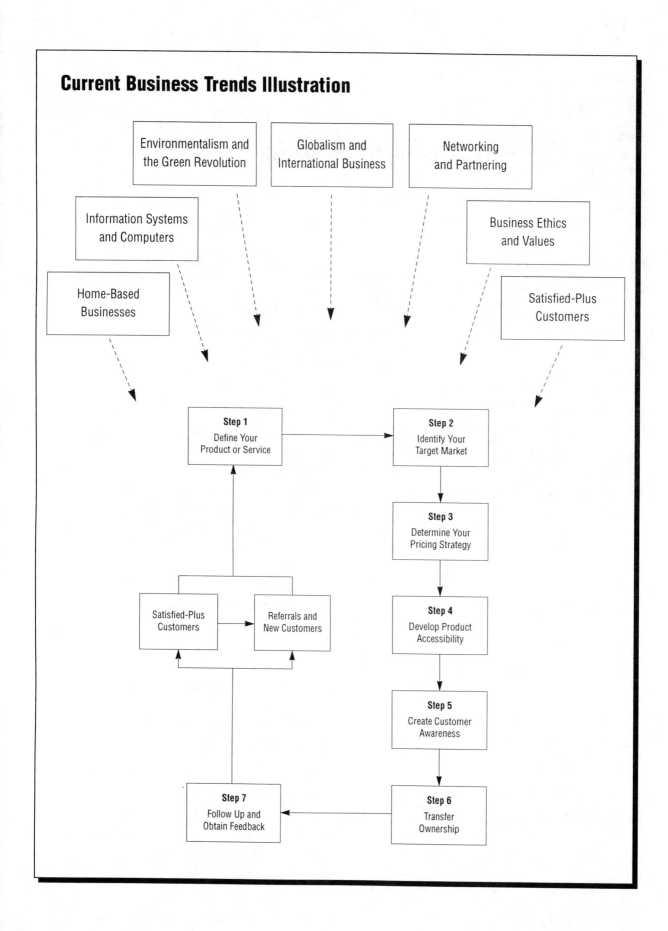

Home business can maintain low overhead by using an answering machine, fax, or computer in place of an office staff. By using the place you live as your business' physical facility, you can enter a market slowly, try different methods of selling, or experiment with the product before spending a large amount of money on start-up costs. Home business can also provide low-cost training for entrepreneurs-to-be who work at another full-time job while they build up a business or make extra money — which for many families has become a necessity.

Day care providers, painters, bookkeepers, consultants, auto mechanics, tutors, software developers, and writers are just the tip of the home office revolution. The home business trend is significant both as a way you can do business and as a potential market for your products. You need to consider how dynamic the home-based business trend is.

For example, garage sales are a common form of home-based business. Although they are regulated differently in each state, garage sales are often outside the regular taxing structure. Nevertheless, they serve as a definite source of income for hundreds of thousands of people. Some people use garage sales as a one-time opportunity to get rid of a house full of accumulated belongings. Others go from neighborhood to neighborhood joining garage sales to sell their own line of products, from candy to small appliances.

The number of arts and crafts shows, bazaars, fairs, and flea markets is on the rise. They are usually based out of a home, though the marketing element may be a more established business with a permanent location. Items sold at craft shows or fairs are often produced at an entirely different location, such as the manufacturer's garage, shed, or extra bedroom. Art and craft manufacturers can keep overhead low and concentrate their production efforts at the most convenient time, when kids are home or after getting home from another job.

Many people find a definite tax advantage to having a home-based business, whether they take advantage of the home office deduction or not. If you have a room with a separate entrance, a detached facility, or a space used exclusively for your business and as the main place of doing business, you may be able to use the home office deduction. The tax laws change regularly, however, so check with the IRS before taking the deduction.

Information Systems and Computers

Innovations in information systems and computers are having a profound effect on the growth of home-based business and small business in general. One-person operations rely on the computer as secretary, book-keeper, database manager, and with fax and modem, as instant delivery system.

Information is power, and with modern innovations, information is available to anyone who has the technology to access it. You can accelerate product life cycles, production cycles, and product introduction, and make new sales channels available through the television, phone, fax, and computer. You can access a product or product supplier from another country through a computer service you operate out of your home, or from wherever you use your laptop or palmtop computer.

Computers and information systems are revolutionizing the way people do business. Computers allow you to design your own brochure, produce your own book, or start a magazine or a mail order business. You can use interactive programs to write a business plan or loan proposal, or you can do an international search for possible representatives for your product. You can do total market analyses of new areas for your product from your home computer. In addition to how computers change business practices, consider what changes cellular phones and wireless transmission may bring to business communication.

Each new technological breakthrough or innovation spawns hundreds and possibly millions of products and businesses. Some will replace existing products and businesses, some will add to them. For how many businesses will the computer serve as a transportation, delivery, or advertising medium using modems or fax modems? As the possibilities unfold with on-line bulletin boards and the Internet, you can tap new markets with new products and new technologies.

How will information systems affect you — either your actual product or how you market it? As computers in homes become as common as telephones, what effect will they have on how people shop and how you get their attention? You need to make the terms user-friendly, voice activation, infomercial, internet, and usenet, among other popular new phrases, part of your ever-expanding computer-era vocabulary.

Environmentalism and the Green Revolution

Recycle, reuse, don't waste, save the forests, and watch the landfills. Pollution must be cleaned, lowered, and avoided. Watch your health and the health of the planet. The ozone layer needs protection. These buzz words send a clear — and clean — message. The U.S. consumer is undergoing an environmental consciousness raising.

If you are testing your product on animals or endangering a species, the customer will get you. You need to consider what effect America's environmentalism will have on how you package your product, deliver it, dispose of it, or determine its composition. How will you dispose of the waste created when you manufacture your product? How does by-product waste disposal affect the price of your product? These are important issues to consider in today's business world.

Globalism and International Business

The international arena is affecting all stages of the marketing process. As new markets open, international demand grows for products for which demand has declined in the United States. Tourists bring tastes for new ideas and new products back to their home countries, influencing the direction of national and international marketing.

For example, espresso is a favorite in France. The founder of Starbuck's Coffee thought Seattle consumers might develop a taste for espresso, then expanded to market Starbuck's espresso nationwide, and eventually worldwide. Now French espresso drinkers can sample American-made Starbuck's espresso. In the process, thousands of people are employed, in France and in the United States.

You can tap into other business trends to help you take advantage of global markets. You can use information systems to access international marketplaces and potential customers or product sources via computer without leaving your home or office. You can use networks or partnering arrangements to act like, and get the benefits of, big business without losing the advantage of being small. Using and combining these dynamic competitive edge trends will help you make the most of your marketing process.

Networking and Partnering

Small businesses have always relied on a heavy dose of networking to build their critical word-of-mouth marketing channels. However, small businesses have also learned that it is possible to tap into the benefits of being big by either partnering or joint venturing with a big firm or getting together with other small firms through industry and professional associations and organizations. You can use other marketing channels and offer other product lines to your existing customers and expand your customer base through networking and partnering. You can share databases, acquire new software, and combine marketing efforts.

For example, shops in a strip mall can combine their efforts to attract customers to the entire mall rather than to each individual shop. Combining their marketing know-how and marketing dollars — either to buy advertising, improve the attractiveness of the mall, or sell gift certificates good at every shop in the mall — often proves to be much more cost-effective than the marketing any individual shop could afford.

A group of individual craftspeople might hire a sales representative to work for the whole group. Manufacturing networks or marketing networks are growing by leaps and bounds. In sparsely populated areas where people want to work in their homes or on their land, networking with other manufacturers or producers can help develop markets and serve as buying groups to secure raw materials at lower prices, making the venture more profitable. Several artists may work together as a cooperative or form associations specifically to generate leads for the group.

Networking also allows a certain amount of mentoring by bigger businesses to smaller businesses. A small business can hook up with a mentor business almost like an internship. The small business is groomed to work with the big business. The small business works directly with the big business to make certain the product the small business will produce meets the standards of the larger business. Partnerships and alliances are formed that could affect your marketing process significantly.

Business Ethics and Values

In the late 1980s, consumers began to react negatively to what they perceived as shoddy products, poor customer service, and irresponsible business policies. Some companies tried to respond to consumers' demand for more ethical business practices. Ben & Jerry's Ice Cream, The Body Shop, and Nordstrom have adopted business values that a significant number of consumers are looking for. A certain percentage of the profit or sales at these companies goes to social causes. If they use cheaper labor or get resources from a developing country, part of the revenue goes to helping the indigenous peoples. Customer service is critical. Nordstrom has had a nationwide impact on how retail business treats the customer. It has set a standard of customer service that has influenced what consumers now expect. Businesses can no longer consider customer service as an extra; they must consider it a regular part of operating costs.

Businesses must also consider multiculturalism and cultural diversity in their approach to business and marketing. These trends affect labeling, pricing, packaging, colors, image, and advertising. You need to consider how this trend toward business ethics might affect your marketing process.

Satisfied-Plus Customers

Customers expect to be satisfied. If you cannot satisfy your customer, he or she will walk away dissatisfied. Even if your customer is satisfied with your product or service, you may not receive an immediate or noticeable response. You have no guarantee that your customers won't be enticed away by a business with a slight competitive edge — anything from contributing to a cause the customer supports, to heading the recycling drive, to importing products that sell for a few pennies less.

Your customers need to be more than satisfied — satisfied-plus — to make your marketing process work. The satisfied-plus customer will stick with you, tell others about your product, and be a cheerleader for your business. Advertising that your donut shop sells a baker's dozen, 13, for the same price as your competitor's 12 will not satisfy your customers. They expect 13, so you need to offer 15, or 13 plus a cup of coffee, or 13 plus an appealing place to eat the donuts. Yesterday's standards of excellence meet today's standards of adequate. Being just adequate will not give you a competitive edge in the long run.

With some products, computers for example, an attribute like user-friendliness is somewhat elusive. When personal computers first appeared on the market, consumers settled for unfriendly computers. When competitors in the computer industry delivered a user-friendly product, consumers moved dramatically to those producers. Every other computer manufacturer had to respond immediately. The case is similar with car manufacturers — when small, fuel-efficient cars came on the market, competitors had to respond or lose their market niches. When customers come to expect something in a product, you must respond to that expectation in order to remain competitive.

Notice that quality is not described as a competitive edge trend. You don't have a choice whether or not to strive for high product quality. If you don't produce a quality product, you won't stay in business. You certainly won't come close to having satisfied-plus customers.

Current Business Trends Summary

Business trends other than the seven discussed here may influence your particular idea or product more directly. As you read this book and develop your marketing strategy, watch for the trends relevant to your business. The trends could impact any part of the marketing process at any time. You can log and track the trends that affect you more specifically on Worksheet 1, Assess the Potential Impact of Current Business Trends, at the end of this chapter.

Understanding the total marketing process is the best insurance you can have that your business will lead the market and grow with your customers. Chapter 3 discusses how to write a product profile, an essential part of Step 1 in the marketing process, defining your product or service.

Worksheet 1 – Assess the Potential Impact of Current Business Trends

Current business trends can affect the successful marketing of your products and services. You need to consider them at each step of your evolving marketing process. Describe here how each of the following current business trends might affect the marketing of your product or service, and what you can do to remain aware of these trends in developing and maintaining a competitive advantage. As you develop your marketing process, refer to your answers here.

Home-Based Businesses _____

_____

_____

Information Systems and Computers _____

_____

_____

Environmentalism and the Green Revolution _____

_____

_____

Globalism and International Business _____

_____

_____

Networking and Partnering _____

_____

_____

Business Ethics and Values _____

_____

_____

Satisfied-Plus Customers _____

_____

_____

Other Trends _____

_____

_____

3 | Develop a Product Profile

Now that you have an overview of the entire marketing process and the types of current business trends that can have a major impact on your success, you need to specifically identify and define just what it is you are selling. What are people buying from you? Have you developed a new idea into a marketable product? Are you offering a new service in your community? Are you selling a product that requires you to provide service or training, such as a new VCR with home-site installation, training, and a six-month follow-up visit to ensure successful use?

How you define your product or service is an ongoing process. You will need to reevaluate your product definition over time, as customers use your product and give you feedback. Developing an initial product or service profile will help you with the remaining steps of your marketing process, including targeting your most likely customers (Step 2), effectively pricing your product or service (Step 3), and developing appropriate customer access to your product (Step 4). Step 5, creating customer awareness of your product or service, also requires that you be specific about what you are selling. You need to define your product for your customers in order to successfully advertise.

Begin, at this early stage in the marketing process, to specifically identify the special features of your product that you will tell your customers about in your advertising. The words and pictures you use in your advertising should attract the customers you want — the ones you identify in Step 2 as most likely to buy your product as you have defined it. You also want to define your product or service so that you can facilitate easy transfer of ownership (Step 6), and easily follow up and obtain feedback (Step 7). As you can see, defining your product and writing a product profile is essential to building a successful marketing strategy that generates the results you want.

Write a Product or Service Profile

A good way to effectively define your product or service is to write an initial product or service profile. You will refine your product profile throughout the marketing process, to focus your market research, to price your product, and to write advertising copy. What specifically are you offering, delivering, or enabling your customer to experience? How will your product give more satisfaction to your customers than they expect, or more satisfaction than your competitors offer for similar goods and services? By answering these questions, you differentiate yourself in the marketplace — you begin to carve out your market niche.

Tangible and Intangible Benefits of a Product

Your product or service profile should take into account both the tangible and intangible aspects of what you are selling. The tangible elements are those that are directly experienced, seen, smelled, tasted, or heard. For a product, you need to identify and describe its physical properties, such as size, shape, weight, color, sound, or smell. You can also include various identifiable performance characteristics, such as its comfort, efficiency, or durability.

The intangible aspects of a product or service are indirectly or subjectively experienced, and involve feelings, perceptions, or impressions. For a product, subjective evaluations might include whether or not the product is fashionable, exclusive, or attractive.

As the chart on page 21 illustrates, you can identify physical properties, performance characteristics, or subjective evaluations of your product or service and transform them into advertising copy. Your goal in writing a product profile is to highlight the special features of your product that distinguish it from the competition. Worksheet 2, Special Features of Your Product or Service, at the end of this chapter, will help you identify what is unique about your product, and what features you think will help you secure satisfied customers.

Tangible and Intangible Benefits of a Service

If you sell a service, you can identify the tangible benefits by describing the purpose of purchasing the service — to improve speaking ability, protect from burglars, or deliver faster. Services can also be described according to performance characteristics, such as regularity, durability, or specialized skill.

Intangible, subjective evaluations might include efficiency, professionalism, or responsiveness of the service provider. Again, the chart on page 21 shows how a service's purpose, performance, and subjective evaluation can translate into advertising copy.

Product Profiling and Market Research

Defining your product and identifying your target market are closely related. People purchase products and services for various reasons. You can use any of those reasons — any of those customer needs or desires — to differentiate your product or service from others in the marketplace. You need to define your product to suit your customers, and you need to target customers who suit your product.

Consider, for example, how Evergreen Indoor Plant Nursery might define its product to suit its most likely customers.

The Elements of a Product or Service Profile

Product

Physical Properties	Size — single serving; industrial strength
	Shape — fits in the corner
	Other — sweet fragrance; excellent tone quality; lightweight
Performance Characteristics	Comfort — doesn't pinch
	Efficiency — gets the job done fast
	Other — precise; stable; stackable; durable; audible
Subjective Evaluation	Fashionable — shows you know today's trends
	Exclusive — available for a limited time only
	Other — feminine; manly; mature; professional

Service

Purpose	Improvement — in speaking ability
	Protection — from burglars
	Other — beauty; pleasure; delivery; problem solving
Performance Characteristics	Regularity — every week
	Durability — lasts a lifetime
	Other — skill; experience; specialization
Subjective Evaluation	Efficiency — in only one day
	Responsiveness — designed with your needs in mind
	Other — informal; courteous; attentive

⇨ Paul and Ellen are the owners of the Evergreen Indoor Plant Nursery. They want to develop a marketing plan, and the first step toward that goal is to write a product profile, to specify exactly what they have for sale. Part of that process is to consider what types of people buy plants and why. How are Evergreen's products going to be differentiated from all the other plants, flower arrangements, shrubs, bushes, and vegetable plants on the market?

First, Paul and Ellen need to describe the physical properties of the plants they plan to feature at the store. When Paul and Ellen conceived the idea, they really wanted to distinguish their nursery by featuring plants that thrive indoors, grow with little maintenance, and complement decor in a home or office. Paul and Ellen think this type of plant will attract a broad customer base and will distinguish their product from high maintenance plants, outdoor plants, and vegetables.

Second, Paul and Ellen need to identify performance characteristics of their product. Because the plants need little maintenance, they are easy to care for. The plants are sold in medium-sized pots, so customers do not need to transplant them — eliminating the need to buy a new pot or soil. Low maintenance is a key performance characteristic of the product.

Third, the plants available at Evergreen Nursery come in rich shades of green and are planted in attractive pots or baskets. The attractiveness of the product will enhance customers' subjective evaluations of the plants.

As the Evergreen Indoor Plant Nursery develops its marketing plan based on the seven step marketing process, it can fill in, for Step 1, the following product definition:

Green plants that thrive indoors, take little maintenance, and come in pre-potted, decorative containers.

Identifying the special features of your product is essential to developing a successful marketing plan. Customer tastes can change so quickly that a competitor may add a bell, whistle, or other feature to a product, or add perceived value in some other way, that you lose existing customers and can't acquire new ones.

As the example of Evergreen Nursery illustrates, you need to profile your product on several levels. Quite likely, Paul and Ellen will need to revise their product profile as they do their market research, develop a pricing strategy, or choose a business location. Perhaps they can add low price, convenient location, or free parking to the profile. Throughout your seven step marketing process, be on the lookout for features that differentiate your product or service from others on the market. Worksheet 3, Define Your Product or Service, at the end of this chapter, provides space for you to write your initial product or service definition.

Define Your Competitive Advantage

As you develop your product or service profile, consider how other businesses selling a similar product or service define themselves and their offering. What is it about your product or service that your competitors lack — why should consumers purchase from you rather than from your competition? Identifying your product's special features will help you determine your competitive advantage, which you can then market more effectively to target customers.

At each step of the marketing process you need to focus on your competitive advantage. When you identify your target market (Step 2), you need to know which other businesses are competing for that same market. You need to know how your competition is pricing so that, when you determine your pricing strategy (Step 3), you will know if you have an advantage at a higher or lower price. When you develop product accessibility (Step 4), you need to know where your competitors are located, how your competitors distribute their product, and how your competitors package their product. Most importantly, when you create customer awareness of your product or service (Step 5), you need to tell your customers specifically why your product is better than the competition.

Worksheet 4, Product or Service Profile: Your Company Versus the Competition, at the end of this chapter, will help you compare all the features of your marketing process, pricing, quality, location, packaging, and channels of distribution, to those of your competition. Return to this worksheet after you have read more about each step of the marketing process if you cannot complete it all now.

Product Profile Summary

Your ideas about what you are actually selling will change with time and customer feedback. Customer tastes and product uses can change as competition and new market trends develop to influence the marketing process. Once you have identified your product's special features, the business trends that can help you beat the competition, and who exactly your competition is, you will have completed the first step in the marketing process.

Now you are ready to continue your market research. Chapters 4–6 discuss important techniques to help you identify your target market, which is Step 2 of the marketing process.

Worksheet 2 – Special Features of Your Product or Service

Check the features that apply to your product or service and then go back and check those features which might go beyond your customers' expectations to create satisfied-plus customers.

Applies to Your Product	Creates Satisfied-Plus Customers	
☐	☐	Experience — as a salesperson, accountant, manager, plumber, engineer, or artist
☐	☐	Personality orientation — outgoing or sales-oriented; internal or research and planning-oriented; mechanical or oriented toward physical results; sincere or striving for customer satisfaction
☐	☐	Reputation — recognition for a specific capability, such as solving electronics, manufacturing, or insurance problems
☐	☐	Wide network — recognized as a community leader; know many people in your community or in a specific industry
☐	☐	Large following — many people think you are an expert in a specific field
☐	☐	Convenient location — downtown; near a bus stop; in a local shopping center or business area; free validated parking with purchase; covered garage nearby; valet service
☐	☐	Credit — 30-day open account; easy-pay plan; lay away; company or bank charge cards accepted
☐	☐	Economical — low prices; discounted merchandise; quantity discounts; special offers; coupons; free gifts; contests; sweepstakes; free trial offer
☐	☐	Delivery service — daily pickup and delivery; delivery when repaired
☐	☐	Fast service — in by 10:00, out by 4:00; one-hour fast photo
☐	☐	Quality — the best; made to last
☐	☐	Guarantees — 180-day unconditionally guaranteed service, lifetime warranty; return policy; money back if not satisfied
☐	☐	Diverse array of products or services — one-stop shopping or service
☐	☐	Higher quality of life — more leisure, less bother, greater comfort
☐	☐	Social contributor — train handicapped or unemployed; one dollar of every sale goes toward specific cause; support low income, homeless, or poor
☐	☐	One-of-a-kind offer — first to offer; exclusive; only outlet available
☐	☐	Special markets — queen- or king-sized; big and tall; petite
☐	☐	Lightweight — material breathes; fewer calories; even a child can lift
☐	☐	Heavyweight — rugged; outlasts the rest; exceeds warranty requirements
☐	☐	Compact — takes up little space; fits under airline seats; fits in purse

Worksheet 2 – Special Features of Your Product or Service (continued)

Applies to Your Product	Creates Satisfied-Plus Customers	
☐	☐	Large — does the big jobs; more trunk space; heavy-duty
☐	☐	Natural — no preservatives; all-natural ingredients; natural fibers
☐	☐	Environmentally conscious — environmentally safe; not tested on animals; recyclable
☐	☐	Imported — the world's finest; found nowhere else; exotic
☐	☐	Made in USA
☐	☐	Good investment or high resale value — always in demand; a classic; income-producing
☐	☐	In vogue — hottest new fashion; latest video game
☐	☐	Personal touch — salesperson knows customers by name
☐	☐	Adds value to customer's investment — landscaping; solar heating; insulation
☐	☐	Removes embarrassment — covers the gray; deodorizes; removes wrinkles
☐	☐	Futuristic — the latest in automated equipment
☐	☐	Shows class — good taste; high class restaurant or boutique; appeals to celebrities
☐	☐	Special services or items available — lottery tickets; licenses; bridal registry
☐	☐	Deposit — for recycling; bottle returns
☐	☐	Express service — automated checkout lanes; teller machines; curbside service
☐	☐	Free services included — child care; gift wrapping; delivery
☐	☐	Free lessons — at your home or in our store; on-site training classes
☐	☐	Installation — included with purchase
☐	☐	Mail order services — save the sales commission
☐	☐	Ship anywhere free — buy on vacation, receive it when you arrive home
☐	☐	Competition — meet or beat competitors prices with this ad
☐	☐	Other special features (write in)

_____

_____

_____

_____

_____

Worksheet 3 – Define Your Product or Service

Before reading any further, define here in your own words specifically what you are selling. What special features of your product or service do you want to emphasize to potential customers? How would you describe those special features in your advertising or packaging?

Note that by the end of this book, your initial definition of your product or service may have changed as you learn to master the marketing process. Nonetheless, defining your product is essential to successful marketing, and writing an initial definition here will help you with the remaining six steps.

_____

_____

_____

_____

_____

_____

_____

_____

_____

_____

_____

_____

_____

_____

_____

_____

_____

_____

_____

_____

_____

_____

_____

_____

Worksheet 4 – Product or Service Profile: Your Company Versus the Competition

Compare your products or services to those of your top two competitors regarding the following product or service characteristics. If you cannot complete this worksheet now, return to it after you have read about all the steps in the marketing process.

Product/Service Characteristics	Your Company	Competitor A	Competitor B
Products offered			
Services offered			
Price			
Quality			
Design/styling			
Seasonal/cyclical patterns			
Credit terms			
Hours and days open			
Location of business			
Specific strengths			
Specific weaknesses			
Product/service position			
Media used to advertise			
Type of specialty			
Major way sold (retail, mail order, wholesale)			
Channels of distribution (producer-to-consumer, producer-retailer-consumer)			
Years in business			
Packaging of product or service			
Other characteristics:			

Step 2 – Identify Your Target Market

4 | Target Market Research

The marketing process is ongoing, always requiring you to reassess your product, your business, and your customer. In Step 2 of the marketing process, you will identify your target customers using proven market research and survey techniques.

Market research is the process of gathering relevant information about your current or potential customers, their buying habits, and any special benefits they seek from your product or service. One of the biggest mistakes new business owners make is to target too broad an audience for their marketing campaign. Effective market research allows you to focus specifically on the types of customers who are most likely to buy your product or service. This chapter gives you an overview of market research. Chapter 5 describes some low- or no-cost market research resources, and Chapter 6 discusses how to conduct and interpret market research surveys.

Identify Your Primary Customer Groups

To identify your target market, begin by researching which buyer groups are most likely to benefit from your product or service. Buyer groups are made up of individual consumers with similar needs, characteristics, or buying habits. One type of buyer group might share the need for a long-lasting, value-oriented children's sneaker shoe. This group has a tangible, easily identifiable need that a reliable discount shoe store will probably satisfy. Another buyer group might have a more intangible need, one based on feelings, perceptions, or impressions, such as the need to wear shoes that are trendy or fashionable. A brand name shoe like Nike or Reebok might satisfy these customers' needs.

Clarifying specific market segments, or customer groups, is a critical step in overcoming a rather common problem new small business owners face — achieving a clear market position. You need to understand why people purchase your product or service — what is the product's or service's appeal? Is it the courtesy or personal touch of a salesperson;

the pleasure, efficiency, or safety the product provides; the price, location, prestige, durability, or guarantee offered by your product or your business?

Many small business owners have a tendency to set up shop and take any customer or offer any product or service to get business. Usually, this strategy is neither useful nor profitable. You want to offer a specific product or service and target a specific type of customer. When you do, you will be able to communicate effectively to customers that you have a product or service your competitors do not.

Target Marketing May Require a Geographical Focus

A mobile welder began marketing his new business by leaving his calling cards all over the state of Washington, although he lived in Seattle. He wanted all the business he could obtain, so his schedule was determined by geographic response to his business card. On various days of the week he might travel to towns four hours east of Seattle, necessitating a four-hour drive back in the evening. Several days each week he worked in Bellingham, a town two hours north of Seattle. Some days he left time open to receive incoming calls, which might send him on welding jobs anywhere in the state.

To maintain a locally competitive price for his service, the welder refused to charge travel time for expenses. He was rapidly going broke without more specific geographic targeting for his unique service.

Had this business owner been more specific in targeting a service area, he might have spent money and time to secure local business, and after his business became locally successful, expanded into other areas of the state. By not defining his market, he made inefficient use of his time and resources.

A Lack of Focus Undermines Your Credibility

A superb typist and office manager decided to open her own one-person business in a large downtown office building. She advertised the following services on the front page of her brochure:

> Office Management: Typing by the page, collating, direct mail services, office layout consultant, office space coordinator, photocopying, binding, training for interviewing, collection, EEOC advising, word processing.

That was just a sampling; she would even house-sit. This business owner would have had more success if she specialized her services rather than trying to be all things to all people. At the time, all indications were that word processing would be her best specialty, since it offered her a competitive advantage. However, she could not stand the thought of not going after customers' other needs. She did not take time to check out her competition to determine who might already be providing some of the many services she was competent enough to offer.

Beware of Targeting Diverse Markets at Once

An office supplies and furnishings shop located in a commercial high rise office complex in a metropolitan shopping area tried to target many different types of customers at once with image advertising. The owner wanted to serve the professional offices upstairs, noontime shoppers and lunchgoers who worked in the building and might stroll by, homemakers on the affluent eastside who wanted upper-class home furnishings, a significant group who shopped from out north, and a tour outfit that just happened to unload at the doorstep.

The shop displayed tourist items in the windows — not effectively using the window display for the best target group, the professional offices upstairs. Homemakers were not interested in the tourist items. Professional office furniture buyers did not want to mingle with casual shoppers. The shop's location would have been excellent had it concentrated on one specific target group and focused its advertising. Because the owner did not target a single possible buyer, the image advertising was wasted.

Target Your Most Likely Customer

A frame-it-yourself shop was barely making a profit and decided to diversify. It was a shop catering to a middle-aged, middle-income, mostly female target group. The shop owners, a husband-and-wife team, also sold prepared frames and gave framing lessons. They thought they could target a different type of audience by selling truck licenses to get some additional income. A trucker might walk in to buy a license from the husband while the wife continued teaching her framing class at the front working counter.

The husband was delighted to sell truck licenses because he much preferred dealing with truckers. Unfortunately, the diversification did not enhance the frame business. The owners sold the business rather than put more effort into the target market the business was already set up to serve. The current owners do not sell truck licenses, and the frame business appears to be healthier, due to a closer tie-in with art and photography courses at nearby schools and colleges. The new owners of the shop are focusing their efforts on fulfilling the needs of a specific target group.

Your Business Versus the Competition

Market research also involves researching your competition. Worksheet 4, Product or Service Profile: Your Company Versus the Competition, at the end of Chapter 3, asked you to differentiate your product or service profile from that of your top two competitors. As you do your market research, you want to distinguish your customer groups from the customer groups of your competitors. Good marketing strategy uses what is special about you, your competitive advantage, to attract customers.

To determine your competitive advantage, begin by segmenting your customers into groups with similar characteristics. Then research the buying characteristics of each segment. The Evergreen Indoor Plant Nursery began its target market research by identifying its primary customer groups.

⇨   At the Evergreen Indoor Plant Nursery, Ellen and Paul have identified three main groups of customers who purchase indoor plants and flowers, and each group has particular buying habits. The first group buys plants as gifts. The second group buys plants as decor for the home. The third group buys plants as decor for businesses, offices, stores, hotels, or other commercial sites. Now Evergreen needs to learn how these three main groups compare with the customer groups of its competitors.

One chief competitor is a florist located in a nearby shopping mall. Many local businesspeople shop there after work or at lunch time to buy fresh cut floral arrangements, flowering plants, and small, seasonal houseplants. These customers primarily purchase flowers and plants as gifts. Paul and Ellen do not have expertise in cut flowers. Ellen's interest in college was botany, with a focus on green plants. Paul's background in landscaping dealt with evergreen plants. The nursery, therefore, will probably not target the cut flower or gift markets. Instead, Paul and Ellen plan to target local businesspeople who want green plants for their offices or as decor for their homes or home offices. Paul and Ellen think the home market will be a fruitful one because of the increase in home-based businesses.

The Evergreen Indoor Plant Nursery has now identified its primary customer group, businesspeople who want to decorate their offices and home offices with easy-to-care-for plants. Evergreen knows that targeting this customer group will give the nursery a competitive edge in the marketplace. Evergreen will continue its market research by contacting the Small Business Association (SBA), and by sending out questionnaires to potential customers. These are two forms of market research discussed in more detail in chapters 5 and 6.

When you differentiate your products and your customer groups from those of your competitors, you can make better informed marketing decisions regarding image, packaging, and media selection. Your competitive advantage represents your business' strength to compete in the marketplace.

Identify Your Business' Strong Points

Consider a business' benefits or strengths that help it attract target customer groups in your local area or in your line of goods and services. Generally, the following five strengths separate a successful business from those in the market that are less successful.

- Repeat business — For example, the owner or an employee of a business may have a personal relationship with other local businesspeople to draw them in as repeat customers — the local deli, pub, service station, bakery, or dry cleaners, or a manufacturer's representative or wholesaler who works in the area.

- Recommendations — Many people buy products or services because they receive recommendations from other loyal customers. Once you secure repeat customers, those customers are likely to help advertise your product by recommending it to others.

- Special appeal to certain customer groups — Frequently in business, a particular customer group supports other groups with similar characteristics; for example, women business owners tend to support other women-owned businesses; small business owners tend to buy from small business suppliers or fellow members of a local chamber of commerce.

- Ability to satisfy special needs — Some customers need special services. Grocery stores might offer a special service like grocery shopping to the elderly or shut-ins; other types of businesses might offer free pick up or delivery. If a business can satisfy a customer's special needs, the customer will likely become a repeat customer and even recommend the business to potential new customers.

- Discount pricing — Many successful small businesses, such as co-op membership grocery stores, catalog stores, or discount houses, are able to offer products at lower cost than larger stores can offer because of their higher overhead costs.

One element that is common to all successful businesses, however, is customer satisfaction. In today's market, satisfying the customer is not a choice or a competitive edge. The customer expects to be satisfied. Figuring out what will delight, surprise, or give the added value above and beyond expectation to your customers is a critical ingredient to keeping your targeted customers and getting new ones. What can you offer, deliver, or enable the customer to experience that will give more to your customer than what he or she paid for or expected? Take every opportunity throughout this book, on the worksheets or in the margins, to note how you can more than satisfy your customers. Satisfied-plus customers will be your business' greatest strength.

Focus Your Marketing Goals

Most small business entrepreneurs can better focus on their specific target customer groups by writing a company profile or doing basic market research. As you begin the process of identifying your primary customer groups, consider writing a company profile or goal statement, or filling out a target market analysis like the one on Worksheet 5, Target Market Analysis Questionnaire, at the end of this chapter. This exercise can help you focus your marketing efforts.

The process of writing a company profile or goal statement not only helps you narrow your marketing focus to the group most likely to buy your product, but it also helps employees understand your marketing and sales goals and any investors recognize your goals and whether you are likely to achieve them.

⇨ Paul and Ellen are in the process of applying for a loan to increase inventory and expand the business. They would like to demonstrate to the bank that they have a viable customer base for their product. Paul and Ellen decided to assemble a target market questionnaire — a question-and-answer form that would focus on customer demand, the factors that lead to a customer's decision to buy, and the influences of location, brand name, and price on the purchase decision. A copy of their target market questionnaire is at the end of this chapter.

To begin the process, Paul and Ellen did some preliminary research of the market by asking questions of friends, passers-by at the business location, suppliers, and other shop owners and competitors so that they could see the business from the market's point of view. Their findings in general indicated that the nursery's market is the community in which it is located, though there is some indication that the business could develop to include mail order. Some research also indicates that businesses might be interested in a consultation service in which the owners visit an office or other commercial site and suggest particular plants to complement the architecture and decor, minimize odor and maintenance, and maximize air quality inside the office. Also, there is some demand for a service that provides plants and takes care of them.

Chapter 6 discusses in more detail how to conduct a customer survey. However, even as a preliminary scan of customer tastes and buying habits, you can begin to narrow the focus of your product offering and marketing campaign by asking questions of friends, business owners, and competitors. A target market questionnaire, such as the one Paul and Ellen used, can give you a head start in writing a company profile. A blank version of the questionnaire used by Evergreen Indoor Plant Nursery is included at the end of this chapter as Worksheet 5.

Finally, read below how Paul and Ellen began an initial draft of their company profile. By the time they reach Step 7 of the marketing process, they will be able to refine the company profile to highlight all the most marketable aspects of the business.

⇨ Evergreen Indoor Plant Nursery Company Profile

The nursery specializes in low-maintenance, indoor plants ideally suited for offices in homes and commercial sites. We offer professional consultation for individuals and companies who wish to include indoor plants as part of their interior decorating. Our goals are to:

- Sell quality, healthy plants that will bring our customers good results for many years;
- Provide the highest level of customer service; and
- Conduct follow-up care to ensure healthy, long-lasting plants our customers can enjoy.

With more than ten years of experience in both interior decorating and landscaping, we are uniquely suited to assist our customers in choosing the plants that complement their homes, offices, and lifestyles.

Evergreen Nursery focuses on providing in-depth instructions for the care and maintenance of the plants, or contracts to provide such maintenance, so that our customers will continue to have good results years after their purchase.

As you can see from the example above, Paul and Ellen will need to consider many more aspects of their business, product, and customer before they will have a complete and thorough company profile. In Step 3, they will consider price, and in Step 4, they will consider distribution, location, and packaging. Nonetheless, it is always a good idea to begin putting your company goals on paper. Worksheet 6, Draft a Company Profile, at the end of this chapter provides space to begin writing your company profile.

Target Market Research Summary

Determining who your target customers are is essential to successful marketing. Market research of various kinds can help you identify the personal characteristics and buying habits of your target customer groups. Target market research, Step 2 of the marketing process, needs to continue as part of your successful marketing strategy. As your customer base grows and changes over time, you can keep abreast of new market demands and changes through continued research.

As you continue with your target market research, try to consider how price, distribution, location, and packaging might affect your customers. Chapters 5 and 6 discuss in greater detail how to conduct low-cost, effective market research.

Sample Target Market Questionnaire – Evergreen Indoor Plant Nursery

1. **What benefit is the customer seeking?**

   Decorative, low-maintenance, indoor plants – must be attractive, healthy, long-lasting, odorless. Related products – pottery, baskets, interior decorating consultation services, follow-up service.

2. **What factors influence demand?**

   Customers' knowledge of how to care for plants; price; space available to display plants; number of sunny spots in home or office.

3. **What functions does the product or service perform for the customer?**

   Adds attractiveness to home or office; plants can serve as air filters, especially in offices with no windows that open. May enhance customer's feeling of social responsibility – influenced by rising public awareness of environmental issues.

4. **What are important buying criteria?**

   Price; attractiveness; level of maintenance required; whether the customer can provide best environment for the plant – sun, shade, warmth, or other factors; customer's past experience with owning plants or with dealing with the nursery.

5. **What is the basis of comparison with other products or services?**

   Price; availability of plants in the right size or of plants whose needs, such as sun or water, fit what the customer can provide; availability of training, advice, or follow-up service to help the customer care for the plants.

6. **What risks does the customer perceive in the purchase?**

   The plants might get diseased or die; people might be allergic to the plants.

7. **What services do customers expect?**

   Advice in choosing the best plants to fit the customers' needs.

8. **How do customers decide to buy?**

   Find plants that they feel confident will survive, will complement the decor of the plant's future home, will be easy to care for, and are priced right.

Sample Target Market Questionnaire – Evergreen Indoor Plant Nursery (continued)

9. How long does the buying process last?

Varies: some people buy plants impulsively, especially if the plant will serve as a gift. Sometimes the buying process takes a long time – the customer researches various types of plants, chooses ones that suit the desired location, and comparison shops to find the best price.

10. How much time and money are customers willing to spend?

Many customers will be willing to spend more time to find the right plant because they fear having the plant die if they do not get one they can adequately care for. Customers are not likely to want to spend too much money for fear that if the plant dies the money was wasted.

11. How much do customers buy? How frequently?

Some customers will make one large purchase, particularly if they are buying to fill an office or another commercial site; other customers will only buy one plant at a time, two or three times per year.

12. When does the customer decide to buy?

Varies – impulse buyers will decide the day of or a few days before shopping for the plant; larger purchasers shopping for an office building or hotel will decide that plants are needed well in advance of the purchase, and the customer will shop around for several days, weeks, or even months before deciding where and what to buy.

13. Where do customers seek information about the product or service?

Impulse buyers will look in the Yellow Pages, notice the store in their neighborhood or near their place of work, or rely on word-of-mouth recommendations. Larger purchasers will rely on word-of-mouth recommendations and on print ads or other types of advertising.

14. What kind of location attracts customers to buy?

Shops local to customer's home or place of work; some customers buy plants through mail order.

15. Why do customers choose one brand or service outlet over another?

The nursery has a convenient location or gets good word-of-mouth advertising; good price; customers have a favorable experience with the product or service.

16. Who occupies the market segments identified in questions 1–15?

Impulse buyers live or work near the nursery who want a plant for their home or as a gift; large purchasers include interior decorators, business owners, and office managers.

Worksheet 5 – Target Market Analysis Questionnaire

Fill in the following target market worksheet for your business. Whenever possible, apply the features of your product or service that you identified in Worksheet 2 to help clarify your market segments (see page 24 and 25).

1. What benefit is the customer seeking?

_____

_____

2. What factors influence demand?

_____

_____

3. What function does the product or service perform for the customer?

_____

_____

_____

4. What are important buying criteria?

_____

_____

_____

5. What is the primary basis of comparison with other products or services?

_____

_____

_____

6. What risks does the customer perceive in the purchase?

_____

_____

7. What services do customers expect?

_____

_____

8. How do customers decide to buy?

_____

_____

Worksheet 5 – Target Market Analysis Questionnaire (continued)

9. How long does the buying decision process last?

_____

_____

_____

10. How much time and money are customers willing to spend?

_____

_____

_____

11. How much do customers buy? How frequently?

_____

_____

12. When does the customer decide to buy?

_____

_____

_____

13. Where do customers seek information about the product or service?

_____

_____

14. What kind of location attracts customers to buy?

_____

_____

15. Why do customers choose one brand or service outlet over another?

_____

_____

_____

16. Who occupies the market segments identified in questions 1–15?

_____

_____

_____

Worksheet 6 – Draft a Company Profile

Although you are only at the initial stages of your marketing process, this is a good time to draft a company profile or goals statement. Try to outline as closely as possible what you think your product is and who your customers are. Rely on your answers to worksheets 2, 3, and 4 which asked you to define your product or service, identify its special features, and compare it to the products or services of your competitors.

As you proceed with the marketing process, you will refine your company profile to account for price, distribution, location, packaging, and other elements. In the concluding chapters of this book, you will have an opportunity to refine your company profile and to write a more detailed goals statement for your business.

_____

_____

_____

_____

_____

_____

_____

_____

_____

_____

_____

_____

_____

_____

_____

_____

_____

_____

_____

_____

_____

_____

_____

5 | No-Cost Market Research

You can conduct market research in many ways to learn more about your target customer groups. This chapter discusses how to perform indirect, informal research using materials relating to your particular industry. Chapter 6, Research Survey Techniques, discusses how to conduct direct research of your market using direct observation and questionnaires, controlled experiments, focus groups, and direct mail. For more in-depth coverage of formal market research and use of market research specialists, consult The Oasis Press' *Know Your Market: How to Do Low-Cost Market Research.*

Before launching a marketing campaign, you can use local, public resources to examine the feasibility of success in your chosen market. Reading materials and computerized information network services are tremendously effective — and cost-effective — research sources. Indirect market research sources, such as newspapers, public libraries, and chambers of commerce, provide demographic and other types of information about your target market, which in turn helps to guide the rest of your market research and your marketing efforts to make them the most efficient and least expensive possible.

Researching Public Resources

Many public resources and public service agencies in your community can help you understand your industry and identify your target market segments. You need to know the demographic characteristics of your target market — age, income, gender, education level — and measure the potential demand for your product or service. The research sources described on the following pages are just a sampling. Space is provided throughout the chapter for you to identify resources for collecting data. Worksheet 7, Information Sought in Your Target Market Research, located at the end of this chapter, provides space for you to gather information you can use throughout your marketing process.

Newspapers

Newspapers are an ideal source for market research. Many daily and weekly newspapers can provide information for their metropolitan area by census tract. They may also be able to provide maps showing the geographic concentration of various business activities, such as shopping centers, supermarkets, and recreational areas. By using the data files and readership statistics of newspapers, you can gather information about the demographic characteristics of your target market, such as age, gender, marital status, or average household earnings, and business activity information, such as competition or general economic climate. Combine all this information to identify the characteristics of customers most likely to buy your product or service, to develop a market survey questionnaire, or to select the best papers to advertise in.

Many daily newspapers have a special weekly geographical section. Neighborhood areas may have their own weekly newspaper or shoppers' tabloid. If you intend to locate in the publication's area of coverage, you will probably find the newspaper eager to share its research statistics with you to lure you in as a potential advertiser.

Newspapers

Daily or weekly newspapers and neighborhood newspapers that can help you with your research include:

_____

_____

_____

Public Libraries

University or public libraries are some of the best places to start a feasibility study for a majority of business products or services. Libraries have an abundance of information about business trends, industry trends, specific studies published by consumer research groups, marketing surveys, and a copy of valuable information furnished through government agencies, chambers of commerce, and other organizations. Key publications that can assist with your marketing research include:

- *Census of Business*
- *Census of Population*

- Company annual statements
- *Encyclopedia of Associations*
- *Key Business Ratios*
- *Standard and Poor's Industry Surveys*
- *The Survey of Buying Power*
- Various U.S. Small Business Administration (SBA) publications

---

Public Libraries

Local public or university libraries include:

_____

_____

_____

Government Resources

Government publications, particularly those offered by the U.S. Department of Commerce and the SBA, are extremely valuable sources of information about your target market characteristics. The Department of Commerce can provide census data and industry-by-industry sales statistics. The Department of Commerce's Franchise Company Data contains a wealth of information about franchises, such as capital required, financial management, and training assistance. The SBA offers valuable services to the business entrepreneur. You can get practical marketing information from many of the aids they have published. They also conduct monthly seminars on a broad range of small business topics. Their services and publications are either free or cost very little.

Government Resources

Government resources and publications that you can consult include:

_____

_____

_____

Small Business Administration (SBA)

The SBA's Service Corps of Retired Executives (SCORE) and the Active Corps of Executives (ACE) offer free consulting services and assistance in doing business with the federal government, if the government is one of your target customers. Contact your nearest SBA office to set up an appointment, or call for an SBA free publication list.

The SBA's Small Business Institutes are in more than 500 colleges and universities in the United States. Students team up for college credit to do analysis and make recommendations. In several cities, the SBA now has a business Information Center or Small Business Development Center (SBDC) with a wealth of computer databases, hard data, and human assistance available.

The Evergreen Indoor Plant Nursery is doing some market research by calling the SBA to speak with a SCORE counselor about pricing. Pricing will be an important part of Evergreen's overall marketing strategy, and Paul and Ellen want to get advice from some small business experts.

⇨   To do some research on pricing methods for Evergreen's new consulting service, Ellen called the SBA. A SCORE counselor described how interior decorators price their consulting services as a package deal, and suggested that Evergreen could do the same. If a customer wants to purchase both the consulting service and plants, Evergreen could offer the consulting service at $250, and credit half or all of the price of the plants. Both Paul and Ellen like this idea but want to ask other businesspeople and customers their reactions. Paul and Ellen decided to research further before making a decision on pricing the consulting service.

The SBA has a computer bulletin-based system that allows you to download free information about loans, minority programs, and many other topics and calendars of events at local SBA offices. Call 800-697-4636 for both 2400 and 9600 Baud Modems.

Small Business Administration

Telephone number of local SBA, SCORE office, and Small Business Institute:

_____

_____

_____

Banks

Banks are a natural source for information about the local business climate. They may also have a research and statistics department which could prove helpful. If you convince a loan officer who handles small business accounts that you are a potential bank customer, you will probably gain access to much of the relevant information the bank has available.

Banks

The bank and the loan officer you are dealing with are:

_____

_____

Chambers of Commerce

Joining the local chamber of commerce is one of the best networking techniques for small business owners because its membership is composed of other entrepreneurs in the local community. Many chambers have monthly publications of general business interest and host monthly meetings for sharing the successes and problems of being a small business owner or manager.

Chambers of Commerce

Telephone number of the local chamber of commerce is:

_____

_____

Trade Associations

Of the more than 5,000 trade associations that exist in the United States, one is very likely to be aligned with your specific product or service. Check in the *Directory of Associations* or *Encyclopedia of Associations* at your local library for the address of the closest associations connected with your business, then visit them or write to obtain relevant information such as industry sales, marketing surveys, and forecasts.

Trade Associations

The trade associations relevant for your business are:

Name: _____

Address: _____

_____

Telephone: _____

Contact person(s): _____

_____

Researching the Competition

You will always learn more about your own business when you research your competition. You want to learn what niche competitors are targeting and decide whether you will have more success trying to break into that same niche or targeting an entirely different customer group by using different types of advertising or by varying your product or service slightly.

Yellow Pages

A good source of printed information about your competition is your local Yellow Pages or business phone directory. Read the Yellow Pages under the headings related to your product or service. Consider how your advertising might differ from that of your competitors, particularly if you plan to advertise in the Yellow Pages. What types of customers are other businesses targeting in their ads? Where are the businesses located? These are all important questions in your endeavor to better understand your target market.

Yellow Pages

Which businesses can you identify in the Yellow Pages or other business directories that are direct or indirect competitors?

_____

_____

_____

Related Products and Services

Businesses in related services or product lines are also indispensable resources. Suppliers to retail businesses, for example, are often good sources of information on local pricing policies, trends within product lines, new packaging ideas, and the latest technological advances. Of course, talking to your perceived competitors, becoming aware of their advertising, wandering through their stores or service outlets, and getting to know who they choose for a lawyer and accountant will serve you well in attempting to target your market to your business' best advantage.

Related Products or Services

What businesses in related services or product lines can you network with?

_____

_____

What can you learn from them?

_____

_____

No-Cost Market Research Summary

All of these market research sources will help direct your market research efforts. You need to know as much information about your geographical focus, your customers, and your competition as possible to make informed decisions about marketing and advertising. If you have noted throughout this chapter which resources will be helpful, you are ready to expand your research efforts. Use Worksheet 7, Information Sought in Your Target Market Research, to compile the market data you gather from no-cost market research sources. Chapter 6, Research Survey Techniques, discusses techniques for taking your market research forward to the next step, direct research surveys.

Worksheet 7 – Information Sought in Your Target Market Research

Now that you have identified in this chapter the information sources you will use in your initial market research, fill in the information you have gathered or will gather. Your market research goals are to identify related industry trends and the characteristics and buying habits of your target customer groups.

Newspapers

Which daily or weekly newspapers did you check with, and what demographic information did you gather about their readers?

_____

_____

_____

Which neighborhood newspapers did you check with, and what demographic information did you gather about their readers?

_____

_____

_____

Public Libraries

Which publications did you consult at the library, and what information about your business or your customers did you find?

_____

_____

_____

Government Resources

Which government resources and publications did you consult, and what information about your business or your customers did you find?

_____

_____

_____

SBA

In your initial contact with your local SBA, SCORE, or Small Business Institute, what information did you discover about your business or your customers?

_____

_____

_____

Worksheet 7 – Information Sought in Your Target Market Research (continued)

Banks

Which banks did you speak to, and what information did you find out about the local business climate, economic forecasts, or forecasts about your particular type of business?

_____

_____

_____

Chambers of Commerce

What services can your local chamber of commerce provide, and which should you use?

_____

_____

_____

Trade Associations

Which trade associations did you contact, and what did you find out from them about your products, your customers, and the prospects for the economy?

_____

_____

_____

Yellow Pages

Which Yellow Pages and business directories do your competitors use?

_____

_____

What do Yellow Page advertising salespeople say about using Yellow Page ads for your product or service?

_____

_____

Related Products or Services

What did you learn from researching businesses in related products or services about pricing, trends, advertising, or the potential for cooperative advertising and promotion?

_____

_____

_____

6 | Research Survey Techniques

Research survey techniques can be very sophisticated and accurate when used properly. As discussed in the previous two chapters, you should first focus your research goals by writing a company profile and researching public resources. However, once you have completed your company profile and indirect research, you can gather more detailed information about your target market by surveying your customers directly.

If you use a combination of survey techniques, you will more easily identify a particular target market, a competitor's product or service mix, and any consumer needs still unmet or unsatisfied by the businesses that exist in the marketplace. Determining as much relevant information as possible about your target market segments and their buying characteristics will facilitate the other steps in the marketing process, such as developing an appropriate pricing strategy (Step 3), location and packaging (Step 4), and media selection (Step 5). You can also use research surveys to get customer feedback (Step 7) and to promote satisfied-plus customers and word-of-mouth advertising.

The information sources described in Chapter 5 can help you segment a target market and clarify the potential demand for your product or service. Most of these sources, however, do not involve interactive market research, which is more expensive, more direct, and often more interesting.

The research survey techniques discussed in this chapter are more direct methods you can use to gather relevant information about the demographics of your target group, such as economic status and spending habits, and any psychological influences you need to consider about your target customers.

Developing a Market Research Survey

Whether you launch a new product or service into the marketplace, add a new feature, or review your target group's satisfaction with your current offering, research survey questionnaires can be extremely useful. The nature of the questions you ask, the experiments you undertake, or the observations you make will depend entirely on what you want to know about target customer groups.

For example, you might ask direct questions about target customers' characteristics, such as age, gender, income, and education levels; about their needs, preferences, and buying habits; and about their degree of satisfaction with your product or service. You can also ask how customers feel about your price, location, packaging, and competitors, and about business trends that may be affecting your business. Through effective and timely market research, you will get a better grasp of your overall market position and marketing strategy.

When you design a market research survey, ask questions that specifically relate to the information you are currently seeking. The Sample Customer Profile Survey at the end of this chapter contains some general types of questions you may want to ask in developing your own survey instrument. Read the sample survey for questions you want to include in your own questionnaire. Modify and add questions you feel are appropriate for your business on Worksheet 8, Your Customer Profile Survey, which follows the Sample Customer Profile Survey at the end of this chapter.

Interactive Research

Market research surveys can be very flexible. Once you assemble a questionnaire, you have several options for conducting interactive research, including:

- Direct observation
- Experiments
- Focus groups
- Direct mail
- Interviews

You may use one or a combination of techniques to help you zero in on the target market segments most likely to buy your product or service. Read about the following research survey techniques and choose those best suited to your market research objectives. Worksheet 9, Using and Interpreting Direct Research Surveys, at the end of this chapter, asks you to describe and interpret the information you gathered through interactive research.

Direct Observation

A very simple and direct approach to conducting a research survey is to go to the location of your business, the business you intend to buy, or a competitor's business and observe buyer characteristics. Look for characteristics such as age, style of dress, and method of transportation.

For example, one entrepreneur who was interested in buying an ice cream franchise and locating in Napa, California, spent one day of every weekend for four months casually standing on different street corners counting the number of people who walked by. She was able to determine the best apparent location for her new business, and to familiarize herself with potential customers and her business environment. To observe both target customers and competition in other ways, you can:

- Observe the local competitors' approaches to selling their products or services at their places of business;

- Count the cars or pedestrians that go by your location or anticipated location at different times of the day and week; or

- Observe whether your location or anticipated location is on the sunny side of the street — for more attractive window shopping — or on the going-home side of the street — for more impulse shopping by customers on their way home from work or school.

Direct Observation

What kinds of information could you find by the observation method?

_____

_____

How would you use this information?

_____

_____

Controlled Experiments

Controlled experiments are another excellent method of direct market research. If you plan your experiment properly, this technique can help you identify target market segments.

For example, you may want to experiment with pricing a product differently at various store locations. You can also conduct an experiment in which you hand out advertising or coupons for a new product and record the number of people who respond by purchasing the item. You can hand out free samples with different prices or packaging to different target groups, with a request for feedback to determine which groups respond most favorably. These types of experiments assure that you select an appropriate marketing strategy for your customer groups, including price, packaging, and media, to get the results you want.

Controlled Experiments

How might you use a controlled experiment in your market research?

_____

_____

_____

Focus Group Interviews

Focus group interviews have gained considerable attention in recent years and have been especially instructive to entrepreneurs who introduce new products or services into the marketplace. In focus group interviews, researchers gather eight to ten people to discuss a particular new product or service while the interview is taped. As an incentive, the researchers offer money or a gift, such as a free sample, to each participant.

For example, one college dormitory group was asked to try out a new haircutting device that had an attachment to vacuum the hair while the device was cutting. The product looked similar to a hair dryer. The interviewers showed the product, described its features and advantages, and then demonstrated it. The interviewers asked the group to brainstorm why they might buy the product or why they would not. Whom did they feel would be the best target customers for this device? What price would be reasonable for the product?

The interview process for the new haircutting device was repeated with a group of married people in their twenties and early thirties with young children. This focus group's only concern was that they might make a mistake while using the product, especially on their children. The entrepreneur learned that he would have to figure out some way to alleviate the fear-of-mistakes factor, or else change his intended target market.

Other businesspeople have successfully used focus groups to explore the feasibility of opening a Japanese soup luncheon spot in an office building, to design an advertising campaign for an auto broker, to explore the feasibility of a home-based accounting service, and to sell preassembled awnings for homeowners. Many entrepreneurs experience positive results from focus groups run by local university business students, as well as professional marketing research studies that involve substantial investment. Focus group studies may prove very useful in your own market research.

Focus Group Interviews

What questions might you ask a focus group if you used one in your market research?

1. _____

   _____

2. _____

   _____

3. _____

   _____

4. _____

   _____

5. _____

   _____

Direct Mail

Direct mail can be expensive, but it can also generate a good deal of information. Direct mail surveys can be developed and tabulated easily by hand or on a personal computer. Computers allow you to generate large databases of prospective customers and target those who respond initially.

Develop a customer survey that you can send to people on a targeted mailing list. You can send it to past customers, target groups in the telephone book, or a group of people obtained from a mailing list company. Many companies specialize in selling mailing lists. If you have a computer, you can often purchase mailing lists on diskette to use with your computer's mail-merge capabilities.

Use the information you gathered using public resources, discussed in Chapter 5, to narrow the scope of people on your mailing list. Offer people an incentive to fill out the survey — a free sample, coupon, or discount for first time use. As people return the questionnaires, your task is to tabulate the results to obtain useful information about potential customers.

Direct Mail

Which mailing lists would be useful to you in conducting market research?

_____

_____

How and where can you get mailing lists? How much do they cost?

_____

_____

Personal Interviews

Personal and telephone interviews are another useful survey method, and may be easier, cheaper, and more efficient for a small company than focus groups or direct mail.

You can conduct personal interviews with questionnaires in hand at your business' location. Combining questionnaires and personal interviews is a particularly useful technique because you can develop eye contact and glean information about potential customers through observation as well as questionnaire results. Write down your observations, perhaps on the back side of the questionnaire. Then tabulate all questions and observations to develop a customer profile.

Personal Interviews

Will a personal interview be useful and easy to obtain?

_____

_____

What customer reactions or characteristics will you look for?

_____

_____

Telephone Interviews

The telephone interview is one of the most frequently used methods of gathering market research information. Using a standardized format, such as the one shown on the Sample Customer Profile Survey at the end of this chapter, you can conduct many interviews in a relatively short period.

Telephone interviewers usually use a list of current customers or customers with the same phone prefix. They have also found that a voice-activated computer is an efficient telephone interview technique. Many market researchers have good results using students in marketing courses at universities, as well as professional telemarketers. Making a few calls yourself can be enlightening and give you a good feel for the information and its usefulness.

Telephone Interviews

What telephone interviewing questions might be useful?

_____

_____

Who would make the phone calls?

_____

_____

How can you follow up?

_____

_____

Research Survey Techniques Summary

To develop a purposeful and successful marketing plan, you need to use your researched information to uncover the best way to reach customer groups that have similar characteristics. For example, ask yourself:

- How many potential customers are in your primary customer group?
- How will you best tell them about your product or service?
- What is your competition doing?
- How will you get certain customers to buy from you rather than from your competition?

When you understand your target markets and your competition, you will be able to make more informed decisions about appropriate product pricing (Step 3), accessibility through location, packaging, and distribution channels (Step 4), and creating customer awareness of your product through media selection (Step 5).

Before continuing to the next section on effective pricing strategies (Step 3), complete Worksheet 10, Customer Profile: Your Company Versus the Competition. This worksheet helps you summarize your target market customer characteristics as you now perceive them and allows you to make an initial comparison with whomever you feel are your two major competitors. As you progress through the marketing process, use this information to help differentiate your product and service offerings from what your competition provides. Always focus on your competitive edge so that you can make more effective use of any differences between you and your competition in attracting potential customers.

Sample Customer Profile Survey

The following is an example of a survey questionnaire that you can use in your market research. The questions should be designed to elicit information about potential customers so that you will be more informed about how to market your product to them. This sample is for retail businesses.

Dear Customer:

Please read the following survey questions and respond by filling in the most appropriate answers that describe you as a buyer.

1. When do you prefer to shop? _____ A.M. to _____ P.M.

2. Which days of the week do you prefer to shop? Which nights?

   Days: ☐ Mon. ☐ Tues. ☐ Wed. ☐ Thurs. ☐ Fri. ☐ Sat. ☐ Sun.

   Nights: ☐ Mon. ☐ Tues. ☐ Wed. ☐ Thurs. ☐ Fri. ☐ Sat. ☐ Sun.

3. How do you prefer to pay?

   ☐ cash or check ☐ store credit ☐ charge card

4. What quality of merchandise do you usually buy?

   ☐ high ☐ moderate ☐ low ☐ sale merchandise

5. What type of store do you prefer to shop in?

   ☐ conventional ☐ service-oriented ☐ high fashion ☐ discount

   ☐ other: _____

6. If you have various problems with your purchases, how do you take care of them?

   ☐ fix it myself ☐ return it ☐ outside repair

7. Who does most of the buying in your family?

   ☐ male ☐ female ☐ children

8. What is the age of your major family purchaser? _____

9. What is your age, if you are not the major family purchaser? _____

10. What is your average annual family income?

    ☐ under $10,000 ☐ $30,000 to $50,000

    ☐ $10,000 to $30,000 ☐ over $50,000

11. What is your education level?

    ☐ less than high school ☐ high school ☐ some college

    ☐ college degree ☐ graduate level

12. Which newspapers do you read most often? _____

    _____

Sample Customer Profile Survey (continued)

12. Newspapers (continued)

Which newspaper sections? _____

_____

13. Which magazines do you enjoy reading? _____

_____

_____

14. Which radio stations do you listen to? What hours do you generally listen? _____

_____

_____

15. Which television programs do you usually watch during the week? _____

_____

_____

16. When you recommend our store to others, what appeals to you most that you want to share by word-of-mouth? _____

_____

_____

17. Please make any additional comments or suggestions. _____

_____

_____

_____

_____

_____

_____

_____

_____

_____

_____

_____

Thank you for your time and assistance.

Worksheet 8 – Your Customer Profile Survey

In the space below, outline the ten most critical characteristics and buying habits you need to know about your target customers. Base some of your ideas on the Sample Customer Profile Survey shown on the previous pages.

1. _____
2. _____
3. _____
4. _____
5. _____

6. _____
7. _____
8. _____
9. _____
10. _____

Now construct your customer profile survey based on the critical characteristics you identified above. Try to formulate approximately 15 questions that you can ask customers that will help you gather the information you need to know about them.

Dear Customer:

Please read the following survey questions and respond by filling in the most appropriate answers that describe you as a buyer.

1. _____
_____
_____

2. _____
_____
_____

3. _____
_____
_____

4. _____
_____
_____

5. _____
_____
_____

6. _____
_____
_____

Worksheet 8 – **Your Customer Profile Survey** (continued)

7. _____
   _____
   _____

8. _____
   _____
   _____

9. _____
   _____
   _____

10. _____
    _____
    _____

11. _____
    _____
    _____

12. _____
    _____
    _____

13. _____
    _____
    _____

14. _____
    _____
    _____

15. _____
    _____
    _____
    _____

Thank you for your time and assistance.

Worksheet 9 – Using and Interpreting Direct Research Surveys

Look again at the ten critical pieces of information you need to know about your customers that you outlined in Worksheet 8. As you consider the types of survey methods outlined in this chapter, describe below how you might use these methods to gather the desired information about your customers.

Using Direct Research Surveys

Direct Observation — How might you use direct observation to gather information about your customers, such as customer demographics, buying habits, or other characteristics? _____

_____

_____

_____

_____

Controlled Experiments — Describe how you would use a controlled experiment to gather desired information about your target market. _____

_____

_____

_____

_____

Focus Group Interviews — How might you design focus group interviews to find the specific information you need about your customers? _____

_____

_____

_____

_____

Direct Mail — Which mailing lists would be useful to you in conducting market research? How will you decide that the list will accurately target your customers? What questions might you ask in a direct-mail survey? _____

_____

_____

_____

_____

_____

Worksheet 9 – Using and Interpreting Direct Research Surveys (continued)

Personal Interviews — How will you decide whom to interview? Who will conduct the interviews? What types of questions will you ask to get the information you need about your customers? _____

_____

_____

_____

Telephone Interviews — How will you decide whom to call for an interview? Who will make the phone calls? What types of questions will you ask to get the information you need about your customers?

_____

_____

_____

_____

Interpreting Customer Surveys

Once you gather information about your customers using one or a combination of the survey methods described in this chapter, you need to interpret the information and apply it to your marketing process. In the space below, describe how the following types of information might affect your marketing strategy?

Demographics, such as age, gender, income, or education level: _____

_____

Customer needs, preferences, or buying habits: _____

_____

Customers' degree of satisfaction with your product or service: _____

_____

Customers' opinions about your:

Pricing: _____

Location: _____

Packaging: _____

Competitors: _____

Other types of information: _____

_____

_____

Worksheet 10 – Customer Profile: Your Company Versus the Competition

Part of your market research includes comparing your customers to your competitors' customers. In the space provided, compare your targeted customers to the customers of your top two competitors with regard to the following customer characteristics.

Customer Characteristics	Your Company	Competitor A	Competitor B
Age range			
Gender			
Education level			
Income range			
Occupation			
Location (neighbors, out of state, via mail order, other)			
Lifestyle/marital status			
Culture/values			
Needs met (business, personal, everyday needs, once per year needs, other)			
Sources of transportation			
Major ways to pay (credit cards, cash, check, other)			
Newspapers, magazines read			
Radio or TV stations listened to			
Other characteristics:			

Step 3 – Determine Your Pricing Strategy

7 | Basic Pricing Formats

Pricing is an important step in your marketing process. When you sell a product, you are not only selling the item, you are selling the price as well. Consider price as part of what you are actually offering your customers.

Prices can affect the purchase decision in ways you might not expect. Price tags convey an image, and it may or may not be the total image you need to make the sale. Consider, for example, a couple looking for an antique clock. When they asked the shopkeeper about the history of one clock, it matched what they had been looking for, and they expected to pay about $850. When they learned that the price was only $250, they were disappointed. They believed the low price indicated something wrong with the clock. Their psychological needs would not be met by buying that antique clock. They expected to spend a certain amount to receive a sense of satisfaction.

This couple was not looking for a bargain. Other potential customers might react differently, thinking the purchase was a great deal. Their bargain-hunting needs would be met. Bargain-hunting customers are a different type of customer than those who want to spend more to feel they received high value for their dollar. Price is the customer's measure of what he or she is willing to pay to receive the benefits associated with the purchase.

How you price your product or service will have a direct effect on your marketing strategy. All too often small businesspeople do not adequately consider the value of their own labor and the time and effort they expend to create a market for the products or services. They tend to undervalue their product when they set a price. You need to develop an effective pricing strategy that allows you to sell your products and services at a profit, or you won't be able to remain in business.

When you develop a marketing strategy for a new product, pay attention to how you classify your product and your buyers before you calculate an initial product price. Steps 1 and 2 discussed how to define your product and identify your target market. Now that you know your product and your buyers better, you are ready to develop a pricing strategy that will assure that your product and your buyers connect.

Determining a Selling Price

Correct pricing decisions are a key to successful business management. Prices influence the quantities customers will buy, which in turn affect total revenue and profit. Two principles govern successful pricing — pricing flexibility and cost-plus-markup pricing.

Pricing Flexibility

Because the marketing process is ongoing and can be affected by new business trends, changing target customers, and different buying habits, you need to learn how to develop a pricing strategy that is flexible and that allows your business to compete effectively and grow.

The best price is the one that will get the most dollars while your product or service is on the market. You can achieve this marketing goal by trying to sell a large volume at a relatively low price, or by setting a higher price and perhaps attracting a correspondingly lower volume of customers. In either case, the price you set will be part of your overall marketing strategy.

Some businesses use a loss leader technique — offering selected goods or services at or below cost to attract new customers to the business or to expose existing customers to new items. Sometimes, however, offering a product or service at a relatively low price may detract potential buyers if they are image-conscious and perceive that a low price implies an inferior product.

Knowing your target customers will help you determine if you should price your product for bargain hunters or image-conscious consumers. For the latter, you may want to introduce a new product at a very high markup on cost to help establish the product as a high-quality, prestige item. Often, the key to keeping a product selling as the market for it changes over time is pricing flexibility and experimentation.

Cost-Plus-Markup Pricing

Many different factors enter the pricing process, and you may use different combinations of pricing strategies at any point in time. Although different pricing formats exist for retailers, service providers, and manufacturers, most pricing for a given product reflects three basic factors:

- Direct costs, which includes labor and raw materials;
- Indirect costs, or overhead, which includes administrative and selling expenses; and
- Profit.

When you develop a selling price that accounts for these three basic factors, your pricing equation looks like this:

Price = Direct Costs + Indirect Costs + Profit

Taking these three factors into account is called using a basic cost-plus-markup approach, a strategy used primarily by manufacturers, wholesalers, and retailers. Some price strategy is based on the going rate, used primarily by professionals, like lawyers and consultants, and by retailers who are trying to meet or beat their competitors' prices.

In general, price reflects many parts of an overall marketing strategy, including:

- What potential customers believe to be the value of the product or service;
- The direct and overhead costs of providing the product or service, unless it is to be considered a loss leader; and
- The product or service mixture — the batch of features that are characteristic of the product or service.

However, other factors influence your pricing decision, such as the nature of the product or service, company policy, competition, business conditions, market strategy, and distribution methods.

In general, you can use a markup approach to pricing that will simplify your price equation.

Selling Price = Purchase Cost + Markup

The initial markup, also referred to as gross margin, is the difference between the selling price and the purchase cost. The initial markup should be large enough to cover overhead expenses and still provide a satisfactory profit.

Markup or Gross Margin = Selling Price − Purchase Cost

Markup or gross margin can be expressed either as a percentage of the selling price, used by most retailers and wholesalers, or as a percentage of cost, used by most manufacturers.

Pricing for Retailers

Retailers primarily use a cost-plus-markup pricing method, but if you are a retailer, you will have some specific concerns as you develop your markup percentage and your overall pricing strategy. Worksheet 11, Pricing Checklist for Retailers, at the end of this chapter will help you isolate some key issues you face in developing a retail pricing strategy.

Percentage Markups and Markdowns

A major step toward making a profit in retailing is selling merchandise for more than it costs you. This difference between cost of merchandise and retail price is called markup, or occasionally markdown.

Most retailers express markup as a percentage of retail selling price rather than as a percentage of cost. They do this because when other operating figures, such as wages, advertising expenses, and profits are expressed as a percentage, all are based on retail price rather than wholesale cost of the merchandise. If you research industry standards to learn what other businesses or competitors are using for markup, be sure to find out if their markup is on retail price or on cost.

To express markup as a percentage of retail price, rely on these two formulas:

Dollar Markup = Retail Price – Cost of the Merchandise

$$\text{Percentage Markup} = \frac{\text{Dollar Markup}}{\text{Retail Price}} \quad \text{(as a percent of Retail Price)}$$

Consider the example of a retail garden hose. If the garden hose costs the retailer $6.50, and the retailer thinks customers will buy it at $10.00, the dollar markup is $3.50 ($10.00 – $6.50). Going one step further, the markup as a percent of retail price is 35% ($3.50 ÷ $10.00).

If you expressed markup as a percent of wholesale cost, your percentage would be much different, even though the end result, a markup of $3.50, would be the same. Markup as a percentage of wholesale cost is expressed in the following formula:

$$\text{Percentage Markup} = \frac{\text{Dollar Markup}}{\text{Cost Price}} \quad \text{(as a percent of Wholesale Cost)}$$

In the same garden hose example, the percentage markup is now 54% ($3.50 ÷ $6.50). Retailers customarily express markup as a percentage of retail price, but you need to make sure you know how other businesses are expressing markup so you can be consistent. If the garden hose retailer wanted to compare his or her markup to competitors' markups, the garden hose retailer would need to know if competitors are expressing markup as a percentage of retail or wholesale cost.

If, on the other hand, you know your cost and desired markup, you can determine an appropriate retail price using the following formula:

$$\text{Retail Price} = \frac{\text{Dollar Cost}}{(100\% - \text{desired percentage markup on retail})} \times 100$$

The garden hose retailer estimated a retail price, knew the cost of the item, and then calculated the markup as a percentage of retail price. However, in another example, a toy shop owner purchased a line of tricycles from the manufacturer that cost $60 each. Her research from industry resources and from other retailers showed that a 40% markup, expressed as a percentage of retail price, would usually cover selling expenses and still provide a satisfactory profit. To calculate the retail price, based on cost and percentage markup, the toy shop owner's price on tricycles looked like this:

$$\frac{\$60}{(100-40)} \times 100 = \frac{60}{60} \times 100 = 1 \times 100 = \$100$$

In this example, the retailer would probably want to reduce the price to $99.95 to accommodate customer buying psychology. As discussed later in this chapter, sometimes odd-ending prices suit customers' needs better than even-ending prices. Generally, the opposite is true for service business, as discussed in Chapter 8.

Be sure when you are calculating markup that you take into account all the elements that go into the cost of the item. For example, if you routinely pay $6.50 per garden hose, but add an additional $0.35 per garden hose to transport the product to your store, you should include that transportation cost as part of the total cost of the item. If you calculate a markup you think will provide you with an adequate profit, but fail to take into account all the different elements that go into the cost, you will not achieve the profits you expect.

Ideally, if you research your market carefully and consider all the factors necessary in determining an appropriate markup, all your products should sell at their original retail prices. This ideal rarely occurs, however, so certain price adjustments are necessary to move merchandise, and these adjustments are called markdowns.

Usually, retailers tentatively decide on what percentage must be marked down to excite customers. For example, if you think a 25% markdown will be necessary to sell a lavender sofa, the dollar amount of the markdown is calculated as follows:

Dollar Markdown = Off-Retail Percentage x Previous Retail Price

Dollar Markdown = 25% x $500 = $125

The markdown price is the dollar markdown subtracted from the previous retail price. Hence, the sofa would be $375 after taking the markdown.

If you need to implement a markdown strategy, be sure to consider the wholesale cost of the product. This is not to say that a markdown price should never be lower than cost; on the contrary, a price that low may be your only hope of generating any revenue from the item. But cost should be considered to make sure that below-cost markdown prices are the exception in your outlet rather than so common that your total profits are really hurt.

Calculating Planned Initial Markup

You can decide on an initial markup in two ways. First, you can research the industry and the competition to see what markups other businesses are using. With that information in mind, you can then assess the demand for your product, guess what price you think customers will be willing to pay, and calculate the markup. Alternatively, you can look at the profit picture of your own business and calculate what markup you need to cover expenses and produce a profit.

No matter how much you depend on what competitors are doing or what customers are spending, look inside your business and take into account sales, expenses, and profits before setting a price. Your initial markup must be large enough to cover anticipated expenses and reductions and still produce a satisfactory profit.

The figure is calculated with the following formula:

$$\text{Initial Markup Percentage} = \frac{\text{Operating Expenses} + \text{Reductions} + \text{Profits}}{\text{Net Sales} + \text{Reductions}}$$

Reductions consist of markdowns, stock shortages, and employee and customer discounts. The following example uses dollar amounts, but the estimates can also be percentages. If a retailer anticipates $94,000 in sales for a particular department, $34,000 in expenses, and $6,000 in reductions, and if the retailer desires a $4,000 profit, initial markup percentage can be calculated as follows:

$$\text{Initial Markup Percentage} = \frac{\$34,000 + \$6,000 + \$4,000}{\$94,000 + \$6,000} = 44\%$$

The resulting figure, 44% in this example, indicates the initial markup needed on the average to make the desired profits.

Nature of the Merchandise

While the above formula can be very useful in determining an initial markup, you need to keep in mind that some product lines have much different characteristics than others, and therefore require a different initial markup. For example, a clothing retailer might logically have different initial markup figures for suits, shirts and pants, and accessories. You may want those items with the highest turnover rates to carry the lowest initial markup. You may also want to give products with a shorter lifecycle a higher markup. For example, very fashionable clothing will often carry a higher markup than basic clothing, such as underwear, because the particular fashion may suddenly lose its appeal to consumers.

Demand-Oriented Pricing

The importance of price on overall sales depends on the specific product and on the specific target customers. Some customers are very price-conscious, and others care less about price than about convenience and knowledgeable sales personnel. If you conduct detailed market research (Step 2) and customer follow up (Step 7) you may be able to judge what your customers are willing to spend on your product. You can then base your pricing strategy on customer demand, rather than simply on cost-plus-profit.

This kind of demand-oriented pricing is a powerful alternative to cost-oriented pricing. In the cost approach, a predetermined amount is added to the cost of the merchandise. In the demand approach, price considerations depend on what customers are willing to pay. You base prices on the number of units you think customers will demand at various price levels.

As a retailer trying to develop a demand-based pricing strategy, you might set your floor price as the cost of merchandise, and your ceiling price as the level above which customers will not buy the product. Demand-based pricing requires a good deal of experimentation and flexibility. Consider this example at Evergreen Indoor Plant Nursery.

⇨ This winter at Evergreen Indoor Plant Nursery, Paul and Ellen decided to experiment with selling living Christmas trees. They thought it might capitalize on a recent trend they had noticed in the community. The local paper had run in the opinion page an article opposed to the killing of turkeys and trees for the holidays. The article had generated a tremendous amount of feedback at the newspaper, mostly inquiring about alternatives. Evergreen took out an ad in the paper advertising its living Christmas trees.

Paul and Ellen were able to purchase some young trees at a reasonable price. If their hunch was correct, they could price the living trees well above what cut trees were selling for, because demand for living trees was likely to be very high. They began by selling the trees for $50 each, a 100% markup on retail, considering the cost of purchasing the trees, transporting them to the nursery, and caring for them while they were for sale. The advertising generated a considerable amount of interest, but the nursery made few sales initially because the price was so far above the cost of cut trees of similar size. Paul and Ellen tried to alter their pricing strategy by negotiating with customers who found the price too high. Gradually, they dropped the price to $35 and were able to sell most of the trees at a reasonable profit.

In this example, Evergreen Indoor Plant Nursery attempted to price its product based on customer demand. This kind of policy required experimentation and flexibility. It also required that the nursery follow a store policy of negotiating with customers.

Store Policies

Store policies are guidelines indicating appropriate methods or actions in different situations. If established with care, they can save you time in decision making and provide for consistent treatment of shoppers. Having calculated an initial markup figure, you could proceed to set prices on your merchandise. But a decision as important as pricing should not be rushed. Instead, consider additional factors that suggest what the best price would be. Specific pricing policies you might consider include:

- A one-price system, in which the same price is charged to every buyer of a product, versus the alternative of negotiating price with customers;
- Odd-ending prices, such as $1.98 or $44.95;
- Multiple pricing, such as 2 for $8.50;
- Price points and price zones — for example, all merchandise is priced at either $5.00, $7.50, or $10.00;
- Loss leader offerings — for example, pricing one item well below its actual cost to bring customers into the store; and
- Periodic special sales.

Sale prices and loss leaders may mean little or no profit on these items. Still, they contribute to total profits by bringing in shoppers who may also buy some regular-priced and profitable merchandise, and by attracting new customers. Avoid featuring items that require a large amount of labor, which in turn would reduce or erase profits. For example, shirts would be a better special sale item than men's suits, which often require free alterations.

Supplier and Competitor Considerations

Two factors that you cannot directly control, suppliers and competitors, can severely affect your pricing strategy. In past years, a supplier could control retail prices by refusing to deal with nonconforming stores — a tactic which may be illegal — or by selling to you on consignment. The law changed several years ago to assure that retailers can have final pricing authority.

How your prices compare with your competitors' is a pricing factor you must constantly monitor. Some businesses employ a full-time comparison shopper to assure that their prices are comparable to competitors' prices. You must watch competitors' prices so that your prices will not be too high or too low without good reason. Of course, you may have a good reason for out-of-the-ordinary prices, such as seeking a special price image.

Some businesses follow a policy of selling at prevailing market price levels, called a price level strategy. Selecting a general level of prices in relation to competition is a key strategic decision. The alternatives are an above-the-market strategy or a below-the-market strategy. When commercial airlines engage in fare wars, they are following a price level strategy — when the competition temporarily lowers its prices, other businesses must do the same.

The Business Environment

In addition to suppliers and competitors, other factors in the marketplace affect your pricing strategy. In particular, you need to be aware of how economic conditions, pricing laws, and consumerism might affect your pricing strategy.

For example, consumers tend to be more price-conscious when the economy is depressed, suggesting that you may need to use lower-than-normal markups to be competitive. On the other hand, shoppers are less price-conscious when the economy is booming, which would permit larger markups on a selective basis.

Secondly, you also need to consider the sales practices laws in your state. Make sure your prices comply with any current state or federal statutes. For information on current pricing laws, consult your attorney.

Finally, you need to consider how your potential customers feel about pricing. Do your customers feel comfortable negotiating price, or do they want consistent prices, clearly displayed. Depending on your product and your target market, you may need to consider several different potential customer reactions to your pricing strategy.

Basic Pricing Formats Summary

Because consumers may react differently to how you price your product, pricing is a vital part of any marketing process. Many elements go into developing a pricing strategy. As a retailer, you need to remind yourself how many different decisions go into pricing. Worksheet 11, Pricing Check-list for Retailers, will help you consider all the various pricing decisions discussed in this chapter.

If you are a service provider or manufacturer, or include some of these activities in your retail business, chapters 8 and 9 discuss various pricing formats and pricing variables for service businesses and manufacturers.

Worksheet 11 – Pricing Checklist for Retailers*

This checklist should be especially useful to a new retailer who is making pricing decisions for the first time. Established retailers, however, including successful ones, can also benefit. Use this worksheet as a reminder of all the individual pricing decisions you should review periodically or in training new employees who will have pricing authority.

Yes No

☐ ☐ Is the relative price of this item very important to your target customers?

☐ ☐ Are your prices demand-oriented, based on the level of demand you think exists for your product?

☐ ☐ Have you considered what pricing strategies would be compatible with your store's total retailing mix — including merchandise, location, promotion, and services?

☐ ☐ Will you accept trade-ins as part of the purchase price on items?

☐ ☐ Do you know how your direct competitors' prices are set?

☐ ☐ Do you regularly review competitors' ads to obtain information on their prices?

☐ ☐ Should your overall strategy be to sell at prevailing market price levels?

☐ ☐ Should you ever match competitors' temporary price reductions?

☐ ☐ Have you estimated sales, operating expenses, and reductions for the next selling season?

☐ ☐ Have you established a profit objective for the next selling season?

☐ ☐ Given estimated sales, expenses, and reductions, have you planned your initial markup?

☐ ☐ Is it appropriate to have different initial markup figures for various lines of merchandise?

☐ ☐ Is your tentative price compatible with your established store policies?

☐ ☐ Will a one-price system, under which the same price is charged every purchaser of a particular item, be used on all items? The alternative is to negotiate with customers.

☐ ☐ Will odd-ending prices, such as $1.98 and $44.95, be more appealing to your customers than even-ending prices?

☐ ☐ Will customers buy more if you use multiple pricing, such as 2 for $8.50?

☐ ☐ Should you use any loss leader offerings — selected products with low, less profitable prices?

☐ ☐ Have you considered the characteristics of an effective leader offering?

☐ ☐ Should you use price lining, the practice of setting up distinct price points, such as $5.00, $7.50, and $10.00, and then marking all related merchandise at these points?

* This pricing worksheet has been adapted from SBA Aid #158: "A Pricing Checklist for Small Retailers" by Bruce J. Walker, Associate Professor of Marketing at Arizona State University, Tempe, Arizona.

Worksheet 11 – Pricing Checklist for Retailers (continued)

Yes   No

☐   ☐   Would price lining by means of zones, such as $5.00–$7.50 and $12.50–$15.00, be more appropriate than price points?

☐   ☐   Will you use cents-off coupons in newspaper ads or mail them to selected customers?

☐   ☐   Would periodic special sales, combining reduced prices and heavier advertising, be consistent with the business image you are seeking?

☐   ☐   Do certain items have greater appeal than others when they are part of a special sale?

☐   ☐   Have you considered the impact of various sale items on profits?

☐   ☐   Will you issue rain checks to customers who come in for special-sale merchandise that is temporarily out of stock?

☐   ☐   Are handling and selling costs relatively high due to the product being bulky, having a low turnover rate, or requiring much personal selling, installation, or alterations?

☐   ☐   Are relatively large levels of reductions expected due to markdowns, spoilage, breakage, or theft?

☐   ☐   Will customer services, such as delivery, alterations, gift wrapping, and installation, be free of charge to customers? The alternative is to charge for some or all of these services.

☐   ☐   If your state has an unfair sales practices act that requires minimum markups on certain merchandise, do your prices comply with this statute?

☐   ☐   Are economic conditions in your trading area different from other local or national economic conditions?

☐   ☐   Are the ways in which prices are displayed and promoted compatible with consumers' call for more straightforward price information?

☐   ☐   Are additional markups called for because wholesale prices have increased or because an item's low price causes consumers to question its quality?

☐   ☐   Should employees be given purchase discounts?

☐   ☐   Should you give any groups of customers, such as students or senior citizens, purchase discounts?

☐   ☐   When markdowns appear necessary, have you first considered other alternatives such as retaining price but changing another element of the retailing mix or storing the merchandise until the next selling season?

☐   ☐   Have you made attempts to identify causes of markdowns so that you can take steps to minimize the number of avoidable buying, selling, and pricing errors that cause markdowns?

☐   ☐   Has cost of the merchandise been considered before setting the markdown price?

☐   ☐   Have you marked the calendar for a periodic review of your pricing decisions?

8 | Pricing for Service Businesses

Whether your business is solely service-oriented, or sells both products and services, you need to consider some particular aspects to pricing. People who purchase services have a slightly different buying psychology. The tangible and intangible benefits they are purchasing can carry a very different perceived value than the tangible and intangible benefits of a product. As you prepare to price your service, consider how customers might view its perceived value and what kind of expectations they take to the purchase decision.

This chapter describes some pricing methods you can use to price a service, and gives particular attention to how professionals and consultants might price their services. Worksheet 12, Pricing Strategies for Service Providers, at the end of this chapter will help you identify the pricing variables of your particular service offering.

Service Pricing Variables

Just as with a retail or manufacturing business, your service business needs to set prices that will cover direct costs and indirect costs, and provide a profit. Indirect costs are your overhead or administrative expenses. Direct costs are labor and raw materials. In a service business, direct costs are primarily the service provider's wages. As you develop your pricing strategy, you need to decide how your price per unit — a unit being either each hour of service, or the entire, completed service — will cover direct costs, indirect costs, and profit.

Every service your business provides should contribute to overall profit and bear its share of expenses. To assess whether various services are supporting their expenses and contributing to profit, you need a bookkeeping system that keeps track of the costs and operating expenses associated with each kind of service. If the tracking system works properly, the business can allocate direct costs and indirect costs to each specific service — a method called a cost-center approach.

In personal service establishments, some pricing is determined by outside factors, such as direct competitors' prices, or limitations involved in franchise agreements. In some industries, businesses will all use a commonly accepted price for basic services. For example, most dry cleaners charge the same price to clean a lady's plain dress. The price to clean a man's business suit is also a commonly used standard in dry cleaning pricing. From basic standardized services, businesses can set up a price schedule for other standardized services. They then price special services according to the amount of labor required, often reflected in a flat service fee.

If your business does not have a community or industry standard on which to base your prices, you can develop other methods to cover direct and indirect costs, including the multiplier method and the flat rate approach.

The Multiplier Method

When a service is provided for which there are no community standards, service businesses use a method to allocate indirect costs called the multiplier method.

To determine the multiplier you will use for pricing, you need to divide your total sales by annual labor costs. If you are a new business just starting out, you will need to estimate to get these figures. If you estimate, based on forecasts, that you will have annual sales of $50,000 and total direct labor costs of $30,000, you can calculate your multiplier as follows:

$$\text{Multiplier} = \frac{\text{Total Sales}}{\text{Annual Labor Costs}} = \frac{\$50,000}{\$30,000} = 1.67$$

Next, to calculate the price to charge a client for a job which took three hours, the average worker's wage is multiplied by the number of hours that the job took and by the indirect cost multiplier. For this example, assume the average wage is $15 per hour.

$$3 \text{ hours} \times \$15 \times 1.67 = \$75.15$$

If your estimates in calculating the indirect cost multiplier are accurate, this figure should cover indirect, or overhead, costs and include a profit. To that amount, $75.15, you would add the direct cost of materials used for the job, for example, $13.25. The total job price is billed to the client at $88.40 — $75.15 for labor, plus $13.25 for materials.

The Flat Rate Approach

Several types of service businesses use flat rate pricing — price lists suggested by the manufacturers or price-reporting services, such as those used by plumbing and heating contractors. Repair shops often rely on flat rates. The flat rate is calculated by figuring a standard time to do the job, multiplied by an average wage rate, times a multiplier — similar to the multiplier discussed in the previous section.

Rate = Standard Job Time x Average Wage x Multiplier

The numbers used in this calculation are averages. Businesses using this approach usually assume that the indirect cost-to-sales ratios are the same throughout a particular service industry. If you have much higher overhead, you may have to increase your multiplier. If the local wage rate in your area is higher or lower than the published list for your industry, you should substitute it for the rate in the published list.

For example, assume that a particular job takes two hours, the average wage rate is $7.50, and the multiplier is 3.0. The job would cost: 2 x $7.50 x 3 = $45, which covers your direct labor costs, materials, overhead, and profit. You would then price your service at a flat rate of $45, no matter how long it ultimately takes to complete the service.

⇨ As Evergreen Indoor Plant Nursery plans how to add consulting services to its list of products, Paul and Ellen have decided to charge a fixed rate for the three-part service, which includes:

- A meeting with the client;
- A visit to the site where the plants are needed; and
- A written report of the number and kinds of plants recommended.

For the first year, Ellen plans to be the only person on the small staff who will provide the consulting service, so she will only take into account her salary as the direct cost of providing the service. Ellen has figured her salary at $30,000 per year, or $15 per hour. Market research and sales forecasts have led Paul and Ellen to predict sales of $45,000 for the coming fiscal year. If Paul and Ellen use an indirect cost multiplier of annual sales divided by annual labor costs, the result is a multiplier of 1.5. If each part of the three-part service takes one hour, the pricing calculation looks like this:

3 hours x $15 x 1.5 = $67.50

However, to suit the buying psychology of their customers, Paul and Ellen want to charge a rounded figure, so they will round up to $75 per consultation service. Customers seeking a consultation service will expect to pay a round number like $75, and the higher figure will assure the nursery of a better profit margin.

Ultimately, the price you choose will take into account many other considerations in addition to the cost-plus-profit margin. You need to consider your customers' buying psychology, as Ellen did in this example. You also need to consider how your competitors are pricing their services.

If you are providing a service in addition to an array of other products, you might need to consider what percentage of sales you expect the service to account for, compared to the percentage of time you will spend establishing your business as a service provider. For example, Ellen's consulting services may only account for 15% of sales the first year, but she may spend 25% of her time marketing and selling the consulting service to customers. If that is the case, she may need to adjust her multiplier to cover the additional overhead costs of marketing the service. Ellen might also use some of the pricing techniques of professional consultants, for whom billable hours are often significantly less than the hours they work at building their business.

Professional Services and Consultants

Attorneys, architects, accountants, dentists, doctors, therapists, graphic and interior designers, and other professionals have four primary approaches to pricing:

- By job — This approach features a standardized set fee for tasks like a simple divorce, incorporation, appendectomy, or tooth filling. If performing the service actually takes more time, only the agreed fee is charged.

- By estimate — This approach is determined by the average hours + overhead + materials + profit. Often, the client requires progress reports so that the client is not shocked when the final bill arrives and it is more than the original estimate.

- By hourly fee — This approach is determined by the going price in the community for a professional with similar education, experience, and clientele. The client can keep track of the hours and know the charges as they accumulate.

- By the professional's required hourly income.

If you use the fourth approach, to bill by your required hourly income, you need to consider factors such as billable hours per year, overhead, and levels of responsibility among staff members. For example, if you take two weeks of vacation each year, leaving 50 workweeks per year, and you work 40 hours per week, you can assume that there are 2,000 hours per year that you could bill out to clients.

Most industries standards show that professionals with support staffs consider 80% of their hours to be actually billable or salable, in this example 2,000 hours x 80%, or 1,600 billable hours. Small businesses with an owner or manager who is responsible for everything from marketing, to office management, to public relations, will probably use a figure of 50%, leaving only 1,000 actual billable hours per year. As a professional service provider with relatively low overhead, you might determine your total overhead costs as follows:

Overhead Costs	Amount per Month
Office rent	$400
Phone	75
Secretarial (quarter-time)	400
Supplies	50
Legal/accounting	25
Miscellaneous/mailing	25
Marketing	50

$1,025 x 12 months = $12,300 per year

Given the above overhead costs of $12,300 per year with 1,000 actual billable hours for owner's labor, $12.30 of each billable hour must go for overhead. You need to determine a minimum gross annual salary which can cover these anticipated overhead expenses and provide a livable wage for your services.

Assume you need to earn at least a gross salary of $30,000 a year. You would need to bill clients at $30,000 ÷ 1,000 hours = $30 (your labor) + $12.30 (office overhead) = $42.30 per hour. If you are just starting out, you will probably have a difficult time billing 1,000 hours. If you can charge an hourly fee closer to $45 or $50, you will more easily achieve your earnings goal. However, you may also need to consider less income if the market conditions will not support a higher rate while building your business.

Many consultants look at the overhead estimates and decide to operate out of a home office, which is a fast-growing trend. You can also reduce rent and secretarial expenses significantly by bringing in a partner or partners to share overhead expenses. With some adjustments for costs, such as phone or printing, the same overhead estimate can support the needs of two or three professionals in the same office. By bringing on partners or associates, a professional service provider can reduce the allocation per billable hour that must be included for overhead.

Using the sample figures given above, if you add one partner, you can divide overhead costs in half. You and your partner could each bill at $30 + $6.15 = $36.15, or probably $36 or $40 per hour because service prices are usually rounded up. You may need to try to bill more hours. When the business is new, you will probably spend more time getting clients or new business, which makes it difficult to secure the desired number of billable hours during the first two years.

Pricing a service to adequately cover overhead expenses is one of the most difficult tasks of a service provider. If you undercharge for your time, you will have a difficult time meeting all your expenses and having a livable wage. If you overcharge, you may not be able to compete in the marketplace. Take the time to carefully budget your expenses. Be sure to count travel time to and from meeting with your clients. Consider phone calls to the client, mail, fax paper, and the expense of an online service, if you communicate by e-mail to your clients.

You also need to consider the kind of image your price conveys to your customers. If most service providers in your industry charge by the hour, but you charge a fixed rate, will customers think you will give them a rushed and shoddy job, or will they think you are more efficient or more experienced than other service providers? How will price influence perceived value? Customers often think that the intangible qualities of a service, such as feeling good after a facial, are worth every penny. People seeking advice or consultation services are more likely to accept the advice if they have to pay for it than if it is free. Be sure to include image and perceived value considerations in your pricing strategy.

If you offer a service in addition to a product, such as training on a computer a customer has just purchased, you need to consider how you will price the service in relation to the price of the product. In the case of the Evergreen Indoor Plant Nursery, Paul and Ellen discovered that both the sale of the plants and the consultation service increased when they offered the service as a package deal along with the purchase of plants.

⇨ Paul and Ellen decided that, before they finalized the pricing structure for Evergreen Indoor Plant Nursery's consultation service, they would research how some other consultants price their services. They returned to Step 2 in their marketing process, in which they identified their target market, to research the competition more fully. After some research, Paul and Ellen decided that the consultation service would be more popular among their target customers if it were somehow tied in with the cost of purchasing plants. The final pricing strategy for Evergreen's consultation service became:

For consulting to commercial sites, the flat fee is $250 for an analysis and report recommending specific plants. The fee is fully credited on plant orders from Evergreen Nursery of more than $1,000, and 50% credited against orders more than $500. For orders less than $500, Evergreen Nursery charges the full fee, with a discount on plants and containers of 25%.

In the case of the Evergreen Indoor Plant Nursery, strategic pricing of the consultation service may help to increase the marketability of both the service and the retail products the business sells.

Service Pricing Summary

Successful service pricing demands flexibility and constant monitoring of competitors' prices and customers' moods about pricing. As you develop your pricing method, consider all the different ways you can price your service, from an hourly fee to a per job fee. Worksheet 12, Pricing Strategies for Service Providers, at the end of this chapter, will help you consider all of these important elements to pricing your service.

Worksheet 12 – Pricing Strategies for Service Providers

The following questions will help you outline a pricing strategy that takes into account your competitors, your customers, and the costs of providing your service. Use the space provided to outline a viable pricing strategy.

1. What are some of the methods your chief competitors use to price their service? Do they charge an hourly or a fixed rate? Do they give estimates before they begin the job?

   _____

   _____

2. What method of pricing do you think your customers expect when they buy your service? Do they expect to be given an estimate? Do they expect to be charged hourly, or a fixed rate for the whole service?

   _____

   _____

3. Describe what you think your customers perceive as the value of your service. How can you communicate that value in your pricing strategy?

   _____

   _____

   _____

4. Estimate your direct costs, indirect costs, and profit to calculate an appropriate pricing strategy for your service.

Direct Costs	Labor	$ _____
	Materials	$ _____
Indirect Costs	Rent	$ _____
	Phone	$ _____
	Supplies	$ _____
	Clerical costs	$ _____
	Legal costs	$ _____
	Accounting costs	$ _____
	Marketing costs	$ _____
	Other	$ _____
		$ _____
Profit	% or $	_____

5. Considering all of the above factors, how will you price your service? _____

   _____

9 | Pricing for Manufacturers

Chapters 7 and 8 looked at some of the special pricing considerations of retailers and service providers. If you are a manufacturer, or have some manufacturing capabilities, you may have some additional pricing concerns.

Manufacturers tend to have expenses that wholesalers, retailers, and service providers do not have, such as research and development, tools, and equipment expenses. These are major expenses often incurred at business start-up or expansion, and you need to recoup them over time by factoring them into the price you charge for the product. These expenses are usually factored into overhead, along with the traditional cost factors of rent, legal, accounting, and secretarial services, and other indirect costs.

Manufactured products are generally divided into two broad categories:

- Industrial goods — Products used either to produce other goods or to resell to the final user, such as computer chips, leather, aluminum, or plastic; and
- Consumer goods — Products intended for use by the consumer, such as personal computers, shoes, soft drinks, or plastic rain gear.

Of course, many products can be targeted for sale to both industrial users and consumer groups. Pricing may differ depending on which user group you target, since industrial users often buy in larger quantities and therefore get lower prices from the manufacturer than do retailers and consumers.

This chapter examines some basic pricing formats for manufacturers. It also discusses some particular pricing concerns that will assure that your pricing strategy is customer-oriented.

Floor and Ceiling Prices

In any manufacturing business, various market factors, such as the general economy, technological advances, competition, available resources, and costs, determine both the floor and ceiling price for a given product. The manufacturer must determine a price that at least covers all direct and indirect costs of production and still makes a contribution to profit. This minimum price is called the floor price. However, pricing your product above what the market will bear will greatly diminish sales unless you offer a highly desirable special advantage.

Given this upper pricing limit, how does the small manufacturer price products to cover costs, yet obtain a desirable profit? You need to determine a relevant price range that covers floor costs and stays below the ceiling price.

Unless you conduct the market research yourself, or hire a market research firm, the ceiling price will simply be your best guess, especially if you are selling a new product for which there is no existing competition. It is generally easier to lower prices than to raise them, so you can build in a little extra profit margin at the start as long as the initial selling price will attract customers. Then, gradually lower the price if you feel you have exceeded the ceiling price for that product.

On the other hand, you can use certain formulas to determine the floor price of a manufactured item. The most important part of determining a floor price is to maintain accurate and current cost data. Work with your accountant to calculate specific relevant costs, both direct and indirect. You can use several cost-based methods of pricing, including markup on full cost, incremental pricing, and conversion-cost pricing.

Markup on Full Cost

Markup on full cost is the easiest and most frequently used pricing method among manufacturers. To price an item with this method, the manufacturer determines full costs — labor, materials, and overhead — of a particular item, and then adds a percentage of those full costs as a desirable profit margin. Note that in a retail business, markup is usually figured as a percentage of retail price rather than a percentage of cost (see Chapter 7). In manufacturing, markup is generally a percentage of cost. The calculations for markup on full cost look like this:

Selling Price = Total Cost per Unit + (Desired Markup x Cost per Unit)

Here, markup percentage is somewhat arbitrarily determined, but you should attempt to allocate markup as a percentage of total business overhead costs.

For example, to determine a total cost per unit, you add total direct labor costs per unit, direct materials cost per unit, and overhead costs per unit, as in the example shown below.

Direct Labor Cost per Unit	$0.10
+ Direct Materials Cost per Unit	0.08
Total Direct Cost	$0.18
+ Overhead per Unit	0.04
Total Cost per Unit	$0.22

If management agrees that a 50% markup on total costs would be desirable, then:

Selling Price = $0.22 + (50% x $0.22)

Selling Price = $0.33 Floor Price per Unit

This business could experiment with pricing this product well above this figure, depending on what management thinks the ceiling price is. No matter how high it is priced, however, to achieve a 50% markup on cost, the price should not go below $0.33 per unit. Markup on full cost provides the manufacturer with the highest floor price — a floor price that covers labor, raw materials, and overhead. Incremental pricing and conversion cost pricing calculate markup on something less than full cost, and so produce a lower floor price.

Incremental Pricing

Incremental pricing is used when the manufactured product involves high material and labor costs, but low overhead. The manufacturer may want to determine a floor price which emphasizes the incremental cost of producing additional units — the direct cost.

Selling Price = (Labor + Materials) + Markup x (Labor + Materials)

For example, using the same cost figures from the previous example, the floor price is $0.27 per unit.

Selling Price = ($0.10 + 0.08) + 50% ($0.10 + 0.08)

Selling Price = $0.27 Floor Price per Unit

This approach deemphasizes using overhead in determining the floor price, assuming that overhead costs are minimal or absorbed through a comfortable profit margin on some of the manufacturer's other items.

Conversion-Cost Pricing

Conversion-cost pricing is typical in a manufacturing business in which labor and overhead costs are relatively high, such as machinery manufacturing. The manufacturer bases prices on the value added to each incremental unit. The formula in this case is:

Selling Price = (Labor + Overhead) + Markup x (Labor + Overhead)

Again, using the cost figures from the initial example, the floor price is $0.21 per unit.

Selling Price = ($0.10 + 0.04) + 50% ($0.10 + 0.04)

Selling Price = $0.21 Floor Price per Unit

As you can see from these three different pricing methods, the floor price of a product can vary by as much as 33%, depending on management's emphasis on various cost factors and desired profit margin.

You can affect floor price in other ways besides calculating markup only on labor or materials, and not on other cost factors. One method is to try to reduce costs, and so lower the floor price of your product. If you discover that your product is very price sensitive, you may want to consider lowering costs, so that you can lower your floor price and increase sales.

Price Sensitivity

Your best pricing strategy may be one or a combination of the basic pricing approaches discussed in this chapter. Your pricing strategy may also change considerably over time to achieve maximum marketability for your product. Part of maximizing marketability is to consider how price sensitive your product is.

Many buyers look at price as one of the prime factors influencing their buying decision. Some products and services are very sensitive to changes in price — demand for the product or service changes a great deal with a change in price. If you want to stimulate demand for your product or service and test its price sensitivity, you might experiment by lowering the price to see how it affects sales.

For example, consumer products like sporting goods or clothing are very price sensitive. You can stimulate demand for snow skis in the summer by advertising a one-third off sale and reducing inventories that didn't sell during the regular season. The same applies for seasonal clothing. Some services, like an expensive haircut and facial make-over, are also price sensitive. They may not attract a large clientele unless the normal price is cut considerably or offered on a new-customer-only basis. Price-cutting techniques can develop new target groups for your service in the hope that new customers will like the service and continue to purchase it at the normal price.

Many high priced items, such as luxury goods and medical services, are not usually price sensitive. If Nieman-Marcus marketed its sable coats at a price reduced from $43,000 to $41,000, or increased it to $45,000, the quantity sold would probably not change much. If a doctor offered plastic surgery for half-price, he or she would not likely attract additional clientele, since these services are usually purchased for reasons other than price. In fact, this pricing strategy may even lose customers who would wonder what was wrong with the doctor.

Staple products and many industrial goods are also not very price sensitive. Reducing the price of salt and advertising it as a great deal will probably have little impact on sales since it is inexpensive anyway, is infrequently purchased, and takes up shelf space. Considerably reducing the manufacturer's price of computer chips sold to systems assembly facilities will probably not cause a dramatic increase in sales. The rate of change in technology might make the computer chips obsolete within a few months, and even at half-price they would be useless.

If customers don't purchase according to your initial sales projections, you can experiment with price to determine whether price is a major influence on their buying decision and thereby develop a more appropriate pricing strategy. If you set a relatively high price at ceiling level and the product or service sells well, you have made a good decision. If you need to lower the price to attract customers, you will still need to cover costs and make a profit. You can refine your relevant price range, the range between floor and ceiling price, through trial and error in pricing strategy. To remain competitive, you may have to:

- Lower costs — labor, material cost, or overhead — to lower the price; or
- Accept a lower profit margin.

If the price at which customers can be attracted lies below your floor price, it will not be profitable to sell the product. At this point, you may choose to stop making the product, to manufacture it as a loss leader or to round out a product line, or to differentiate the product on factors other than price.

Differentiate Based on Nonprice Factors

You need to consider several factors when you develop a price strategy for your product or service. Some products can successfully compete on nonprice factors. For example, products that have few substitutions, that are infrequently purchased, or that have low impact on your customers' budget decisions do not rely heavily on their price to be successfully marketed.

To avoid competing with other businesses solely on the basis of price, you can emphasize other features and benefits of your product that may attract customers, even at a somewhat higher price than a competitor's item. Some of these nonprice factors include:

- Advanced technology or design
- High quality or performance
- Packaging differences
- Product availability
- Satisfaction guaranteed
- Service
- Special financing arrangements
- Speed of delivery
- Volume discounts or preferred customer status

In Step 1 of the marketing process, you defined your product with specific attention to how you can distinguish your product from the competition. You also considered your competition during your target market research (Step 2). If you are unable to distinguish your product from the competition based on price, return to the competitive advantages you identified in Steps 1 and 2 to differentiate your product. In particular, look for how you identified buyer and product characteristics and business factors.

Pricing According to Buyer Characteristics

Products can be differentiated by looking at who purchases the product, for what purpose, when, how, and where. Marketers tend to divide products into three categories — convenience goods, shopping goods, and specialty goods.

- Convenience goods are products the industrial user or consumer wants to purchase frequently, immediately, and with minimal effort. Candy, chewing gum, milk, soft drinks, beer, nails, and small machinery parts are all examples of convenience goods. They are usually priced low and sold under many brand names at numerous retail outlets to maximize buyer convenience. The manufacturer promotes the product, or hires marketing intermediaries, such as wholesalers and retailers, to advertise the product.

- Shopping goods are products purchased only after the industrial user or consumer has made comparisons of competing goods based on factors such as price, quality, style, color, brand, and image. These goods tend to be higher priced than convenience items. Promotion is often shared by manufacturer and retailer, perhaps through cooperative advertising. Clothing, jewelry, furniture, appliances, cars, and computers are all examples of shopping goods — the customer will likely shop around before making the purchase.

- Specialty goods are products that possess some unique characteristics that cause the buyer to value or desire that particular brand or style. Original works of art, imported quality items, expensive sports cars, handmade furniture, and customized products are all examples of specialty goods. By advertising unique qualities, manufacturers can command a higher price — often, whatever the market will bear. Consumers and industrial users are willing to pay a high price, go out of their way, or wait a considerable time to acquire these products. Manufacturers frequently use a small number of suppliers or retail outlets for each geographic area in their target market.

If your target customers are looking at your product as a convenience good or a specialty good, they may be less concerned about price than other factors, such as availability in the case of convenience goods, or quality or brand name in the case of specialty goods. If your customers view your product as a shopping good, they may consider price as an important criterion in their buying decision. To minimize this problem, you might try to market your product as something other than a shopping good.

Pricing According to Product Characteristics

The major purpose of classifying your product is to help you focus on your target market and tailor your advertising appeals. You may wish to classify products according to descriptive characteristics, such as:

- Unit cost — The customer's buying decision is affected by perceptions of the product's affordability and quality; a higher price allows you to advertise the product as "top of the line."
- Energy spent getting the item — If little energy is required, you can advertise that the product is convenient or found most everywhere; or you can advertise that consumers can take their time and shop around for specialty or shopping goods.
- Importance or value of the individual item to the consumer or industrial user — Because buying a car or house is more important to a customer than buying a pack of gum, you would use different advertising appeals. You might stress price when advertising the pack of gum, but stress features other than price when advertising a house.
- Rate of change in technology or fashion — Because technology changes more quickly for microcomputers than pencils, you might advertise the technological advances of the computer, but the price of the pencil. Tastes change more rapidly in the teenage clothing market than in fishing attire, so you might price teenage clothing higher and advertise that it is the latest fashion, but price fishing attire lower and advertise that it is a good price value.

- Amount of service, training, or education needed to use the product — Because more training is needed before, during, and after buying a microcomputer than a windup wristwatch, you can advertise that you offer the training on the computer, but advertise that the wristwatch is priced low.

- Frequency of purchase — Because a house is purchased only once or twice in a lifetime, customers may be less concerned with its price than with other issues. On the other hand, a quart of milk or newspaper is purchased daily or weekly, and customers are more likely to be concerned about the price of these items.

How you define your product or identify your target market will have a big effect on your advertising. If you are unable to lower the price of your product, or if your product is not price sensitive, promote other features in your advertising that you know your customers will respond to.

Pricing According to Business Factors

You may consider factors in designing your business' pricing strategy other than cost-plus-profit. Chapter 7 already discussed the possibility of establishing company pricing policies, such as negotiating with the customer. Your business goals or general business economic conditions might also influence your pricing strategy. For example, some of your business goals that might affect pricing include:

- To build a certain price reputation — For example, to underprice your competition so that you can advertise that you won't be undersold;

- To cater to a particular market segment — So that you can advertise that you operate on a sliding fee basis; or

- To compensate for a poor location — For example, to develop a company policy that you will price your product 10% under the better located competition.

Your competition's price policy often dictates your price policy. Over the long run, certain businesses may feel that it is necessary to price according to the competition. A manufacturer or wholesaler of items similar to the competition may have little choice but to price accordingly, whereas a manufacturer of a one-of-a-kind item, or one whose competitor is not in a convenient location, may not have the same concerns.

Some pricing is based on basic economic conditions. If times are good, you can increase profit by increasing prices. If times are bad, you can ignore the standard markup, cut prices, and try to keep your business alive.

Manufacturer Pricing Summary

Developing your pricing strategy is one of the vital steps in your marketing process. Your pricing strategy will fluctuate over time, as costs, market conditions, and target customers change. Pricing needs to cover all expenses associated with providing your product or service and give you an acceptable level of profit for your efforts. Determining both a floor and a ceiling price will help you develop a price range within which you can experiment to see how to best increase sales.

However, you can involve many subjective aspects in your pricing strategy. Pricing can actually influence the development of your target market. A successful pricing strategy will affect your overall revenue and profit picture. As you work on your pricing strategy, consider the following truths about pricing:

It is generally easier to lower prices than to raise them.

You can price your product higher than, equal to, or less than your competition — referred to as "skimming the owner," "me too," and "market penetration" pricing, respectively. Because it is easier to lower prices than to raise them, try the skimming strategy when you introduce a new product or service. Early purchasers of new products tend to have higher incomes and be relatively insensitive to price. As the product or service catches on in the marketplace, you will probably be more profitable if you reduce price to expand your overall target market. For example, a personal computer is now very competitively priced and affordable for a much larger target market than it was in the 1980s, and general demand has increased correspondingly.

Price conveys a certain image or perceived value.

This is an important consideration as you work to price your product to fit your product profile and your target market. For example, discount stores want to convey a certain image when they show retail price with a line through it on their price tags, followed by a lower price designated as "your price." Discount shoppers may think they are getting extra value with the purchase. However, the opposite is also true. If customers are not looking for a bargain, they may attach a negative image to a cheaply priced product.

Most customers are price conscious, but they may not be price knowledgeable.

Customers often do not know the going price for specific goods and services. Higher prices must be consistent with the environment in which the product is for sale and with the product's perceived qualities or features. For example, charging $2.95 per pack of cigarettes may be acceptable for a 24-hour convenience store in the Nevada desert, but it would be too much in a city supermarket. Similarly, the junior partner in a law firm is usually billed out at a lower hourly rate than a senior partner.

High-income consumers tend to be less price conscious.

For the high-income market, low price is neither a valued customer need nor a wise advertising appeal. Individuals with considerable disposable income have more time and money available to shop for specialty goods and services for which the main appeal is uniqueness rather than bargain prices. For example, environmentally conscious or recyclable products can support a higher price because they appeal to customers who are more concerned with environmental issues than price issues.

Charging whatever the market will bear may be an appropriate pricing strategy.

You can price your product or service as high as possible, on a demand basis, especially if it involves emergencies, such as a roadside towing service, tire chains, or all-night gasoline. Also, for products and services of a more unique nature — a commercial artist or custom home designer — it is possible to charge whatever the market will bear. Services like these are customized according to the client's desires and, therefore, are priced according to demand rather than according to a cost-plus approach.

Odd pricing is psychologically preferable to even pricing for manufactured goods.

For example $2.98 versus $3.00; the reverse is usually true for services, $25.00 versus $24.98 per hour. Multiple pricing, 2 for $1.00 versus $0.55 each, can be an inexpensive, yet effective marketing strategy, especially if the customer would normally buy only one item. For a service such as a haircut, a two-for-one pricing strategy may help increase clientele, especially among family and friends. Finally, several well-accepted pricing strategies are called customary pricing, and they tend to build goodwill for the business. For example, rather than increasing the price of a go-cart ride from $1.00 to $1.25 for four minutes, an owner might charge $1.00 for a three-and-a-half-minute ride.

As you can see from this list, many factors go into determining price besides cost. Furthermore, how your pricing strategy influences sales will depend on many factors, including whether or not the product or service is price sensitive, or whether it is intended for an industrial or consumer goods market.

Chapters 7, 8, and 9 have covered many different marketing and pricing issues that are all part of Step 3, determining your pricing strategy. To help you synthesize all of these various issues, Worksheet 13, Target Market Pricing Strategy Summary, on the following page provides you space to summarize the many aspects to pricing your particular product or service.

Worksheet 13 – Target Market Pricing Strategy Summary

In the space provided, describe some of the factors that may go into your pricing strategy. Consider in particular how your targeted customers relate to your product and what type of price will drive them to make the purchase decision.

1. Describe what you think your customers perceive as the value of your product or service.

   _____

   _____

2. How do you classify your product?

   ☐ convenience good   ☐ shopping good   ☐ specialty good

3. How do you rank your product or service in the following categories?

	High	Medium	Low
Relative unit cost	☐	☐	☐
Degree of energy spent to purchase it	☐	☐	☐
Degree of value to the consumer	☐	☐	☐
Rate of change in technology	☐	☐	☐
Degree/amount of training or service	☐	☐	☐
Frequency of purchase	☐	☐	☐

4. Taking into account the pricing formats presented in chapters 7 to 9, estimate your initial pricing formula, including labor, materials, overhead, and reasonable profit.

Labor	$ _____
Materials	$ _____
Overhead	$ _____
Total costs	$ _____
Desired profit	_____ % (of cost or of retail)
Initial selling price	$ _____

5. Your relevant price range is a floor price of $ _____ to a ceiling price of $ _____.

6. What image does your initial price convey to your target customer?

   _____

   _____

   _____

   _____

Worksheet 13 – Target Market Pricing Strategy Summary (continued)

7. Describe how your initial price reflects any extras you provide, such as free delivery, free training, or other special features.

_____

_____

_____

_____

_____

8. To determine your product's price sensitivity, describe how the sales of your product or service would be affected by an increase in price? _____

_____

_____

A decrease in price? _____

_____

_____

9. What factors go into your pricing strategy besides strictly cost-plus-profit concerns?

_____

_____

_____

_____

_____

_____

10. Given your target market, your most effective market pricing strategy could be summarized as follows:

_____

_____

_____

_____

_____

_____

_____

Step 4 – Develop Product Accessibility

10 | Choose a Business Location

Once you have defined your product or service (Step 1), identified potential target markets (Step 2), and developed an initial pricing strategy (Step 3), making your product or service accessible to your target customers is the next important step — Step 4 in your marketing process. Deciding on an appropriate location, the best channels of distribution for customer access, and the best packaging approach for your target customers is essential to achieving marketing success.

Location strategy is closely related to customer demands and buying habits. Location also affects the total product or service image you project into the marketplace. It is, therefore, an important marketing consideration. Distribution strategy is affected by the nature and quantities of the goods and services you provide, as discussed in Chapter 11. Packaging decisions are, in turn, affected by both the image you want to project and the channels of distribution you select, as discussed in Chapter 12. Successful location, distribution, and packaging will assure that your customers and your product connect — the goal of any marketing campaign.

The Elements of Site Selection

The real estate industry often states that the three most important aspects of a business' success are location, location, and location. This is true for many products and services, since customers must be able to access you easily to make it worthwhile to buy from you rather than from your competitors.

If you have a retail outlet, choose a location that is consistent with the image you want to portray. If you want to portray convenience, don't choose a location that is difficult to find. If you are manufacturing a new product, you may want to find a location that is close to your suppliers. If you are providing a service, such as accounting or law, you may want a location that portrays an image of prestige. If you are in the mail-order business, your location should be near a delivery route or central post office where mail can easily reach you.

You need to narrow the factors involved in your site selection. First, choose a particular geographic area, such as the city or countryside, the coast or the mountains. If you do not plan to move from where you live now, this choice is probably already made for you. However, you can give some thought to future relocation or needs for growth. You may want to look at:

- Cost of living;
- Wage levels, especially if you have employees; and
- Real estate costs, both commercial and residential.

You might also consider other variables, such as crime rates, labor relations or unionization, and proximity to colleges and universities. For a complete guide to locating or relocating your business, consult The Oasis Press' *Company Relocation Handbook.*

Once you have chosen your geographic area, you need to choose a district within it, such as a suburban shopping center or downtown business district. Choosing a district for your business involves several marketing considerations, including:

- Street access, if appropriate to your business;
- Opportunities for outside signage;
- Attractiveness; and
- Availability of parking.

If you choose to locate in a shopping mall, you will want to consider the ability of your neighbors to attract your target customer groups. Also, consider your neighbors' willingness to participate in cooperative advertising, discussed in more detail in Chapter 19.

Finally, you need to choose a particular site within the district. Treat renting or purchasing your business location seriously — hire independent inspectors, check all zoning regulations, and have an attorney look at the property lease, if there is one. You should also consider future expansion. Is there neighboring property you can expand into? Do zoning laws allow you to renovate or add on?

How will the particular building or office you choose affect your marketing efforts? Again, consider signage, parking, and the attraction of neighboring businesses. You might also consider whether the building is on the sunny side of the street, or the going-home side. Customers might stroll slowly along the sunny side of a shopping district, but they might also frequently pass by a business near a parking lot, bus stop, or subway station. Are your customers casual shoppers, or other local businesspeople who work in nearby offices?

Marketing is a process that needs constant reevaluation. As you look for your business location, consider how your marketing environment and your customers' needs might change. Be aware of other locations that could serve you as well. For example, when it comes time to renew the lease, consider whether your present location and its associated costs are justified. Consider the element of location as a trade-off with other factors of your marketing mix. Can you justify a poor location that keeps some customers away, but attracts others because you offer low prices due to low overhead costs?

Basic market factors and budget considerations should determine your business location. If your target market is consumers who tend to do a lot of comparison shopping, you may want to locate your business in a regional shopping center. If your target group is the teenage video game market, locate in a local neighborhood site to make your product accessible. A used car dealership may want to locate next to a new automobile showroom to take advantage of customers who are in the market to buy a car. If overhead costs are a major budgeting and pricing concern, consider a home-based business.

The Home Office Option

Although the phrase site selection generally refers to the overall strategy of finding the most suitable location to serve your target market, the 1990s and beyond will be known as the era of the large growth in home-based businesses. This is a major marketing trend and is discussed in Chapter 2. Many small business start ups view the only suitable business site as the home.

However, if you work out of your home or studio, you will have some particular decisions to make that can influence your marketing strategy. Do you want to be open to the public? Will only private clients visit your location by appointment? Will you be open only on certain days or at certain hours? How will these various restrictions affect your business and family life?

You should also consult licensing, permit, and zoning regulations for running a home business in your area. You will probably not encounter any state or local regulations for running a simple office out of a spare room, but more elaborate businesses, with manufacturing aspects or employees, might face some regulations. Ask your attorney about any specific laws that might affect your home business. Also, for a helpful guide to starting and operating a home business, consult The Oasis Press' *Home Business Made Easy*.

Locating Your Service Business

If you provide a service, will customers be coming to you, or will you be going to them? Most retail outlets have customers coming to their location, so it needs to be compatible with the target customers' needs — convenience, parking, and shopping. However, for many services, from a freelance photographer, to a management consultant, to a tree-trimming service, you will travel to your clientele, so office location will be less significant in helping achieve a clear market position.

While having a good location does not guarantee marketing success, it certainly can be a major element in providing many services, such as cleaning, banking, and shoe repair. Offering a high-quality service, but having a poor location can damage the image you project in the marketplace. You will need more advertising dollars to help create awareness of your service, since target customers will be less likely to frequent a poor location.

Business Location Summary

Worksheet 14, Business Location Evaluation, on the next page asks you to evaluate many of the important marketing considerations involved in choosing a business location. It also provides space to summarize any distinguishing features and advantages about your location that lend to customer accessibility. Chapters 11 and 12 continue discussion of product accessibility by evaluating distribution and packaging.

Worksheet 14 – Business Location Evaluation

Rate each of the following location criteria.

	Poor	Fair	Good	Excellent
If you work out of your home, how would you rate its accessibility?	☐	☐	☐	☐
How do you rate consumers' need for your product or service?	☐	☐	☐	☐
How do you rate your location's accessibility to your major customers?	☐	☐	☐	☐
How do you rate how concentrated your potential customers are in your market area?	☐	☐	☐	☐
The community's current level of ability to support your business at your chosen location is:	☐	☐	☐	☐
The community's growth potential is:	☐	☐	☐	☐
Availability of the major kinds of transportation your customer will use is:	☐	☐	☐	☐
Parking facilities are:	☐	☐	☐	☐
How do you rate the local population's demographics (for example, age, income, gender, occupation) with your company's needs?	☐	☐	☐	☐
The desirability of this location in relation to your suppliers is:	☐	☐	☐	☐
The availability and affordability of the type of employees your business needs are:	☐	☐	☐	☐
The flow of passers-by at this location is:	☐	☐	☐	☐
How do you rate how important the going-home side of the street is to your business?	☐	☐	☐	☐
How do you rate how important the sunny side of the street is to your business?	☐	☐	☐	☐
How do you rate how important the attractiveness of your location is to you in terms of living and working in the community?	☐	☐	☐	☐

Worksheet 14 – Business Location Evaluation (continued)

Summarize the distinguishing features and major advantages to your chosen location in the space below.

Distinguishing features of your location:

_____

_____

_____

_____

_____

_____

_____

_____

Desirability of your location compared with your competition:

_____

_____

_____

_____

_____

_____

_____

_____

Major advantages of your chosen location:

_____

_____

_____

_____

_____

_____

_____

_____

11 | Select Channels of Distribution

The whole marketing process involves producing, pricing, distributing, and promoting goods and services to existing and potential customers at a profit — creating satisfied-plus customers. If you cannot successfully distribute your product or service to your customers, all of your other marketing efforts may be useless. You must effectively move your product or service from producer to consumer in a timely and cost-effective way.

Some products or services are more dependent on effective distribution methods than others. For example, an impulse item, like cookies, are purchased primarily on an availability basis. Customers may see many television commercials advertising a brand of cookie, but if that brand is not in the store when the customer decides to buy, he or she will not postpone the purchase. The customer is likely to impulsively buy another brand that is in the store, and your cookie business will lose the sale.

As a business entrepreneur, whether you are a producer or service provider, you must match your ability to produce and supply goods and services with the needs and demands of the various market segments or target groups you have identified.

If your product or service requires you to give special concern to its distribution, you want to include selection of an appropriate distribution system as part of your overall marketing plan. The distribution method you choose can affect other marketing decisions, such as business location, pricing strategy, advertising, and sales promotion. This chapter discusses various distribution methods, and how to choose a method that suits your target market.

The P-W-R-C Channel

Four typical channels of distribution are shown below, varying primarily in the number of intermediaries — the producer, wholesaler, retailer, and consumer — that handle the product.

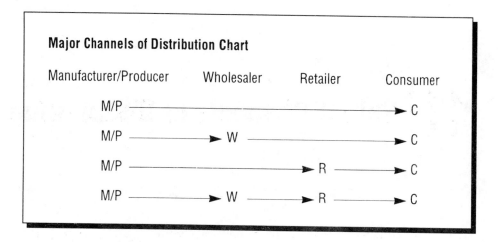

Major Channels of Distribution Chart

Manufacturer/Producer	Wholesaler	Retailer	Consumer
M/P ──────────────────────────────────────► C
M/P ──────► W ──────────────────────► C
M/P ──────────────────────► R ──────► C
M/P ──────► W ──────► R ──────► C

The supply channel you choose depends primarily on your product and your target customers. For example, perishable goods, such as fresh vegetables, require either a shorter supply channel or the use of large-volume, widespread wholesalers to get perishables to the consumer quickly. Other products, such as books, generally pass through a wholesaler and retailer before reaching the consumer, because the producer — the book publisher — cannot support a sales staff with the time or expertise to deal with the millions of bookstore retailers from whom consumers buy books.

Many producers of consumer goods use the producer, wholesaler, retailer, consumer (P-W-R-C) channel because it enables a small company with a limited line of products to use the promotional resources and buyer networks that large wholesalers with broad market access can offer. While this approach to product distribution gives the lowest cost to the manufacturer or service provider — because others take over the distribution and promotion — it also requires you to relinquish control when title of the goods passes to the wholesaler and then to the retailer.

The same producer can use several different distribution channels at the same time. For example, companies such as L.L. Bean and Eddie Bauer may offer goods both directly by mail order catalog and factory outlet. A producer of soap products may distribute through the channel of grocery wholesalers, to food stores, to consumers. The soap company can also share a distribution channel with producers or manufacturers who sell to large retail chains and motels. Amway and Avon, both producers of hygiene products, move their products from the producer, to a network of salespeople, to the consumer.

A jewelry designer may have a studio, where customers can buy direct, but also use large retail department stores throughout the United States and overseas to sell merchandise. The incentive for the customer to buy directly from this type of producer is both the opportunity to meet the artist and the opportunity to buy at a discount.

Marketing your products through catalogs can open up new target markets and supplement retail store sales, or expose the manufacturer to the user more directly. For example, The Sharper Image has opened its market greatly through this effective distribution channel.

Often, small businesses can arrange special supply networks or partnerships to maximize profits. These networks are among the current business trends discussed in Chapter 2 that you should try to take advantage of. Consider, for example, this scenario at the Evergreen Indoor Plant Nursery.

⇨ Evergreen Nursery is primarily a retailer, although it does grow some plants from seed. The owners are very concerned that their products be of high quality, so they purchase most of them directly from producers — bigger nurseries that have the time and expertise to raise healthy plants.

However, to assure that the plants they buy are of the highest quality, Paul and Ellen need to use a broker who visits the bigger growers and hand picks many of the plants Evergreen will sell. The broker adds to the cost of the plants, which tends to make some of Evergreen's plants higher priced than its competitors. Paul and Ellen need to find a way to continue to get high quality plants, but to eliminate the broker from the channel of distribution.

One key supplier is a large nursery located 100 miles north of town. As Paul and Ellen have worked to expand and grow their business, they have developed a very good relationship with this supplier. A sole-source relationship might be worked out with the supplier for certain plants if the supplier could plan its growing seasons with Evergreen's particular needs in mind, but at no additional cost.

This arrangement would require the supplier to grow some plants that it does not currently grow so that Evergreen can stop using the broker for some of its inventory. It is a risk for the supplier because, at first, Evergreen would be its only customer for the new plants. If Evergreen grows as its owners expect it to, the arrangement could be very lucrative for both nurseries.

If Evergreen, in the example above, can make the supply network work, the owners will eliminate excess cost, which in turn allows them to reduce prices while maintaining quality — a major competitive edge for their marketing campaign. Evergreen could take further marketing advantage of this distribution arrangement by advertising that its plants come from one reliable, local source. This type of advertising appeal might impress many potential customers who want healthy plants that will grow and thrive in the area's climate.

Furthermore, a partnering relationship like the one Evergreen and its supplier are trying to work out helps the supplier. The supplier can sell the new plants in its market and may also join in some cooperative advertising with Evergreen, such as joint brochures or other media to promote the products.

Service Distribution

Almost all professional services are distributed from the producer — the professional service provider — directly to the consumer, unless the professional service is subcontracted through a retail organization such as a referral agency. Sometimes a referral agency is the best way to market and distribute your service, but it will probably add something to your price — the referral agency will take a cut of your sales. If most of your competitors use referral agencies, you might be able to undercut their prices by avoiding using an agent. However, your marketing costs may then increase as you try to make customers aware of your service as an alternative to the referral agencies' service providers.

Sometimes, you can differentiate yourself in the marketplace compared with your competition by developing a unique method of distribution. For example, although most services are provided directly to the consumer, the market for a local service such as pet grooming could be greatly expanded by effectively marketing video tapes on the subject through pet mail order catalogs. A local veterinarian equipped a mobile van to make her services more readily accessible to rural customers three days per week and operated out of a regular office for the remainder of the time.

Distribution and Target Markets

Although you can certainly use more than one channel of distribution at the same time, you want to make sure that you are not duplicating your effort and are selecting channels that appeal to different target market segments. You will want to find out which channels of distribution are most frequently used by your competitors, since that often affects your profit margin and the upper limit of what you can charge for your product. If your competitor usually sells directly to consumers through a factory outlet, for example, and you use more distributors that add to cost, you will need to keep your markup relatively low to compete effectively on price factors.

Since everyone involved in the distribution process adds a markup to the product before reselling it to the next person in the distribution channel, you can often gain a better profit margin by eliminating one or more of the typical middlepeople, if this seems feasible. The same product can be sold at several different prices, depending on how many levels it has passed through in the distribution process.

Factory Outlets

One current marketing trend is for factory outlets located in rural communities that cater to a different target customer than its counterpart in urban areas with large shopping centers. Prices at these outlet centers are usually less than in urban areas and cater to the value-conscious customer who will use their time and gas to travel to these centers for the parking convenience and localized comparison shopping readily available. Here, the channel of distribution is from the manufacturer directly to the target customer, rather than through wholesalers who markup products they sell to retail stores. Everyone saves, but the target market segment has to be large enough to warrant a special factory outlet.

Sales Representatives

Many manufacturers use independent representatives to sell their products to both wholesalers and retailers. These salespeople often sell a variety of products that may or may not be similar. For example, many artists in the crafts business and greeting cards industry use representatives who travel a particular geographic territory selling artists' goods to retail stores and specialty shops in that territory. The artists benefit by getting much greater exposure for their goods than they could selling to local stores or selling directly from their studio. They usually pay sales reps 15 to 20% of the sales order for their product.

International Markets

If you want to expand your target market to include international clientele, you will need to consider using special wholesalers and sales representatives, called brokers, who charge a percentage, often 10 to 20%, of the total sale to take care of customers for you. Although you could do this yourself, it is often more practical and financially viable to allow the export-import brokers to handle customer-related distribution aspects. If you want to import goods from other countries and serve as a distributor yourself or sell them from your retail outlet, you will also probably want to use customs brokers who specialize in this distribution function. Chapter 20 discusses international marketing in more detail. You can also refer to The Oasis Press' *Export Now: A Guide for Small Business* for more information on international exporting.

Channels of Distribution Summary

When you perform your market research (Step 2) and customer follow up (Step 7), be sure to investigate which channels of distribution work best for your customers and your marketing goals. Use Worksheet 15, Channels of Distribution, on the following page to summarize how you plan to distribute your products or services. A well-planned distribution method will assure that your product or service is available to your customers when they decide to buy — a vital part of your marketing process.

Worksheet 15 – Channels of Distribution

When you choose a method of distribution, you need to consider your competition, your customers, costs, and the future growth of your business. The questions below will help you outline a viable distribution method for your product or service.

Describe the major channel(s) of distribution your competitors use. _____

_____

_____

Describe the channel(s) of distribution you plan to use. _____

_____

_____

_____

How do your proposed channels of distribution differ from your competitors'? _____

_____

_____

Describe how your chosen distribution strategy might affect sales given your target markets. _____

_____

_____

_____

Who do you specifically plan to contact to set up your distribution network? _____

_____

_____

What percent or profit margin will your distributors charge to handle distribution for you? _____

_____

If you plan to do any importing or exporting in international markets, which brokers will you contact (see Chapter 20)? _____

_____

_____

What percent or profit margin will international brokers charge for handling international distribution for you? _____

_____

12 | Develop Packaging and Product Image

To make your product or service accessible to target customers involves many factors beyond deciding on physical location and appropriate channels of distribution. You need to consider several packaging aspects, both physical and psychological, that invite customers to try your product or service. All these factors together affect the image you portray in the marketplace — your total product image. How you present or package your total image involves a combination of communication tools and becomes an effective part of your marketing strategy.

This chapter discusses various methods for developing and promoting product image, including logo, brand name, and package design. Worksheet 16, Visual Imaging of Your Product or Service Package, at the end of this chapter leads you step by step through designing a total product image.

Visual Communication Tools

Visual communication tools, like logo, location, drawings, or photographs, can attract customers to a product or service. For example, the business environment of a manufacturing outlet, store, or office tells a story and creates an image — hopefully a positive image — in the minds of potential customers. Storefront signage, window displays, and point-of-purchase displays all communicate a certain image, as do the clothes that a salesperson or service provider wears. Three of the most important visual communication tools you possess in translating your total image are your package design, your printed promotional materials, and your product name.

Package Design

One major aspect of your total image is the actual product package itself. The logo, colors, product description, brand name, amount included in a given package size, and the number of different package sizes available are all part of the packaging image you can create. Often, the first opportunity to attract a customer and create awareness of your product or service is your packaging. You also need to consider whether the packaging is accessible for the customer to touch, hear, or thumb through.

How many times have you been attracted to a new product or service because its name, logo, or container caught your eye? International Business Machines (IBM) used its business name in introducing a new product, the IBM Personal Computer. Dress designers have become successful by developing a unique label to which people are often attracted before seeing a particular garment. Children's toys are often packaged in brightly colored see-through packages to attract attention, or in no package at all to let the customer see and feel them, such as stuffed animals.

Carefully consider the impression you want your product to make on customers when they first see it. Should you use garish colors to stand out among the competition on a store shelf? Should you use very classic or elegant packaging to establish an image as a luxury or high-quality product? Should you emphasize environmental awareness in your packaging, such as printing "made from recycled materials" on the sides, to attract an environmentally conscious target market?

Look at your competitors' packaging. How will your product image compare with that of your competition? Perhaps you want your packaging to look similar, to blur the distinctions between your product and the competition and possibly ride on competitors' successes. Perhaps you want to distinguish yourself from the competition, to establish yourself as a new force in the marketplace. These are both legitimate marketing strategies.

Another goal in packaging is to promote your logo or brand name. If you think your product will sell well based on brand recognition, you might want to focus on developing an effective brand logo early on. Your logo will help spread awareness of your product and your business when you use it in advertising, business cards, and other printed promotional materials.

Printed Promotional Materials

As you develop your product image and packaging, you may need to consult a professional graphic designer to design a logo, business card, brochure, or stationery. All of the printed material associated with your business and your product influence and communicate your total product or service image. Simply designing an appealing and attractive business card can make your product and your business feel more accessible to the customer.

If you feel creative and have a specific logo, poster, or flyer design in mind, it can be fun and rewarding to play with your own ideas on paper or on a graphics-based computer program. If you need help or need a more professional design, your local Yellow Page listings can help you find a professional graphic designer. Also, ask other small businesspeople which graphic designer they have used and get a referral to one whose work and logo designs you like.

You also want to consider how your product image is portrayed in other advertising media, such as magazines, newspapers, posters, and billboards. Will you put your logo in every ad? How important will your logo be in brand recognition. Sales promotion campaigns involving contests, prizes, coupons, and free home trials can also be very effective in communicating an image to customers. Will bargain hunters scan the coupon page of their daily paper looking for coupons for your product? Do you want your logo to jump off the page to grab customers' attention? These are all important considerations as you develop your product image and your advertising campaign.

Product Name and Other Descriptive Words

The words you use on your package design or business card are an important part of your marketing campaign. Don't miss the opportunity to spread your marketing message through the words on your packaging or your product name.

The power of suggestion to buy often comes through the words you use in your packaging. Phrases, such as the all-purpose cleanser, express mail delivery, and lawn care specialists, relay important qualities about the product or service to potential customers. The words can also promise intangible benefits to attract the buyer — the perfume with sex appeal, for that satisfied feeling, the drink that makes you feel good all over. In fact, the words on the package, business card, office signage, or logo design can do much to position a product or service in the marketplace. The following are just a few examples of how your product name or description can communicate important information to your customers.

- Location of your business — The Last Chance Cafe, the "last stop for next 27 miles," or Eastside Tavern;
- Target audience of your product — The Adult Game, or "For those who care enough to send the very best;"
- Ingredients used in the product — The Low-Calorie Sweetener, or "all natural;"
- Where the product is manufactured — California's Finest Redwood Furniture;

- How the product is used — "When you don't have time to cook," or "When you need variety;"
- The results of using the product — The People-Pleasing Soft Drink, or "Faster relief for your sinus headache;"
- Guarantees that come with the product — "The only battery guaranteed for the life of your car;" and
- The expertise of service providers — Factory-Trained Mechanics, or Certified Gemologist

Every element of your packaging and advertising should communicate to customers how the product or service will benefit them. Effective target market research (Step 2) focuses your attention on the customer, and helps you view your product from the customers' perspective.

Return to worksheets 2, 3, 4, 6, and 10 in which you drafted your product, company, and customer profiles. These worksheets should help you develop an effective total product image that is engaging and accessible to customers.

Communicating Perceived Value Satisfaction

When you identify and differentiate a new product or service, you choose to try to sell it to particular market segments, and you price it, locate it, and distribute it accordingly. What you are actually selling is a combination of the good or service itself plus various perceived features and benefits in the total purchase package.

The key to good marketing positioning is to define real or perceived differences between products offered in the same market areas. You want to interpret and communicate what sets your product apart and show potential consumers why your product is beneficial to them, especially compared with your competitors. You want to emphasize the perceived marketing advantages of your product as you plan your marketing campaign.

For example, purchasing a piano may include free delivery, free lessons, or a free tune-up. Purchasing furniture might include some interior decorator consulting, free delivery, or color counseling. A personal computer retail store that includes free lessons and on-site follow up with the purchase of a computer system may be more successful in positioning itself in the volatile personal computer market than other computer stores.

The combination of features offered is called your product or service mix. You can develop advertising and media selection that successfully distinguishes your products and services compared with your competitors. If you know your particular product or service mix, you can more easily identify your differential advantage in the marketplace.

Many businesses sell products or services that are nearly the same as their competitors', such as salt, cigarettes, beer, or blue jeans. For example, Jordache brand jeans launched an expensive television advertising campaign to create a teenage target market for expensive designer jeans. These jeans may be undifferentiated from others like them in the marketplace, except for the media advertising promoting the brand-name label. When the actual product is undifferentiated, the perceived product benefits, such as youth, sex appeal, power, or status, become the essence of the total product offering. This total image makes the difference in getting your target customers.

For example, Paul and Ellen, the owners of the Evergreen Indoor Plant Nursery, have chosen a business name and developed product displays that communicate a particular image to their customers.

⇨ The Evergreen Indoor Plant Nursery is trying to develop its product accessibility, Step 4 of its marketing process. As part of their overall marketing plan, Paul and Ellen realize they need a way to demonstrate not only what product they offer — low-maintenance, indoor plants — but also the service they provide. Many people who come to a plant nursery do not consider that the nursery can give advice on interior decorating.

Paul and Ellen made a conscious choice in naming their business that they hoped would communicate to customers the types of products and services they offer — they called the nursery an indoor plant nursery, to emphasize the indoor plants they sell and interior decorating services they offer. However, Paul and Ellen feel that, while the name communicates a significant amount about their products, it does not do enough to advertise their services.

Paul and Ellen have decided to develop a display in the retail section of the nursery — a typical business office, one without plants and one professionally decorated with plants, a before-and-after effect. They have also worked out a partnering arrangement with a neighboring furniture store to set up a similar display at the furniture store, with a sign that reads, "Plants provided by Evergreen Indoor Plant Nursery," and a stack of the nursery's brochures nearby.

Evergreen Indoor Plant Nursery has taken some important steps toward communicating a particular product image. Paul and Ellen identified a target market — business owners — and developed a product image, business name, and point-of-purchase displays that will attract that target market and highlight the product and service features the target market needs and wants.

Packaging and Product Image Summary

As you develop your product image and packaging, the logical next step is to prepare your advertising message — the subject of Step 5, creating customer awareness. Before you move on, however, complete Worksheet 16, Visual Imaging of Your Product or Service Package, at the end of this chapter to develop the communication devices offered by your product image and packaging.

Worksheet 16 – Visual Imaging of Your Product or Service Package

List the special features, benefits, advantages, or intangibles you want to communicate to your potential customers as part of the total image conveyed through your packaging.

_____

_____

_____

_____

_____

_____

_____

_____

_____

_____

How do you plan to increase accessibility of your product or service through total image packaging? Describe the specifics of the following packaging aspects.

Logo: _____

_____

_____

Location: _____

_____

Price strategy: _____

_____

Brand name: _____

_____

Product name: _____

_____

_____

Worksheet 16 – Visual Imaging of Your Product or Service Package (continued)

Special phrase, words, or jingle: _____

_____

_____

Package or container design: _____

_____

_____

Colors: _____

_____

_____

Sizes and quantities available: _____

_____

_____

Label design: _____

_____

_____

Business card design: _____

_____

_____

Business or office signage: _____

_____

_____

Describe how you can differentiate your product from the competition by communicating any perceived value satisfaction to your customers?

_____

_____

_____

_____

_____

Step 5 – Create Customer Awareness

13 | Your Advertising Message

Most entrepreneurs use a variety of advertising and sales promotion techniques to help achieve essential market awareness. Advertising and sales promotion go hand in hand as part of an overall marketing strategy. Through advertising media, such as radio, television, newspapers, magazines, and trade journals, you can attract customers to you. Sales promotions, coupons, direct mail flyers, publicity, public relations, personal selling, and point-of-purchase displays can be effective communications tools to turn interested potential buyers into actual customers. Creating customer awareness of your product or service through your advertising message and media alternatives is Step 5 in your ongoing marketing process.

Chapters 13 and 14 discuss how you can create customer awareness by developing an effective advertising message, and by choosing the most appropriate advertising media. Advertising will be one of the most costly parts of your total marketing process, and so a media cost comparison is also included as part of Step 5.

Several worksheets are included as part of Step 5 to help you develop your advertising message and identify appropriate advertising media. Worksheet 17, Planning an Advertising Message that Supports Your Total Image, at the end of this chapter applies all the work and research you have done so far, in Steps 1–4, to writing a powerful and effective advertising message.

A Purposeful Advertising Message

Advertising and sales promotions are designed to:

- Sell;
- Identify the company and its product or services;
- Present product features or benefits that will appeal to target customers;
- Identify the place and price of the goods and services;
- Offer specials, such as product samples, two-for-one sales, or reduced prices, in an effort to attract customers or deplete inventories;

- Attract new customers and generate support among existing customers;

- Keep a trade name fresh in customers' minds until they need the product or service again;

- Promote your marketing advantage, distinguishing your company and its products or services from competitors;

- Build confidence, promote goodwill, and speed up inventory turnover; and

- Reinforce customers' need for your product or service.

Your message influences the buying decision and affects your overall marketing image. People often buy promises they have seen advertised somewhere. They buy to satisfy perceived needs, solve problems, or satisfy a desire. Your advertising message should communicate an image of your product's benefits — desirable personal qualities your customers will exhibit if they buy your product, such as integrity, caring, or budget-consciousness, and perceived tangible or intangible benefits of the product or service, such as rich texture, sex appeal, or healthiness.

Your advertising message should respond to the proverbial customer question, "What's in it for me?" If your advertising message successfully communicates qualities or benefits customers are seeking, it should arouse a desire in your potential customers to purchase the advertised item.

Advertising Total Image

You can develop advertising messages that support the total image of your business and the package of goods and services you are providing. Keep in mind that the following images are important to consider as you develop your advertising message:

- The perceived value of your product or service to your customers;

- Your personal and organizational sales goals and image;

- An up-to-date profile on the buying and lifestyle characteristics of target customer groups; and

- The tangible and intangible benefits of using your product or service.

When dealing with intangible benefits, it is especially useful to create mottoes, metaphors, and picture images that the intended customer can easily remember. Consumers of intangible goods and services often don't know the quality of service they are receiving until something goes wrong. It is up to you to remind them what they are getting — to spell out the perceived benefits by using creative pictures and words.

Advertising Message Content

You can effectively develop your advertising message in many ways so that it reaches your target customers. Your advertising message needs to be relevant to the target customers by specifying benefits that say: "My friends or family will gain something if I buy it." The advertising message can also communicate immediate benefits to potential customers, such as offering them specials, a free home trial, lifetime guarantee, or "the best that money can buy."

Keep the message simple and direct, since potential customers only have a few seconds to observe. People are constantly bombarded with advertising from all directions in the course of a single day. An unusual ad will attract attention better than a long or complicated one. Readers, listeners, and viewers often gloss over ads that don't strike them immediately. Ad layout that is simple and direct — that spells out specific benefits — and utilizes a dominant element that people can focus their attention on will attract attention easily.

Arousing people's interest and desire is often best accomplished through the use of words and images that arouse emotions — fear of being robbed if you don't have enough insurance; love if you smell good or wear the right clothes; success if you carry a leather briefcase or have a personal computer at the office. Avoid exaggeration and words that are overused, too generalized, or dishonest, and don't make specific claims that can't be demonstrated. Use words and images to create a concept of honest value that will justify the price.

Effective headlines and sub-headlines, along with catchy phrases and tunes, symbols, or special effects, can create a lasting image in the consumer's mind. However, clever headlines that try to trick the imagination or deceive can backfire, so try to be creative without being difficult. Creative use of leading questions, unusual or catchy headlines, and headlines relating to local news or personalities can catch customers' attention. Avoid distracting techniques, but try to use demonstrations whenever possible to get audience or reader participation and involvement.

The image you project through your advertising copy is reflected in the ad copy choices you make, including benefit-words, print size, colors (black print on white background is most effective), or typography (Olde English projects antiquity, heavy black print often indicates a bargain in the offering). Be sure to effectively use white space — the areas of your advertising space that have no pictures, words, or sound. People remember ad copy better and more vividly if the total ad space is not filled with words.

Testimonials are great word-of-mouth advertisements and can be effective, especially when the commercial is presented by a well-known personality who lends a certain character to the advertising image. However, be sure such a personality remains popular and in favor with the target audience you want to reach.

Don't forget essentials such as the company name, phone number, address, and brand name or logo. If your brand or logo is well-recognized through previous advertising efforts, it makes sense to include this factor in the message to build trust, confidence, and continuity in an overall image.

And, finally, ask for the sale — close the sale with customers after familiarizing them with your product or service benefits by asking them to "send check or money order," "act now," "write now for free information and coupons."

You may want to design the advertising message yourself, appoint an employee or associate to handle that task, or even hire an outside advertising agency to help bring the message to the target groups with a degree of professionalism. If you are interested in developing your talent along this line, you can find a host of books, seminars, and tapes available that will teach you how to develop this skill. Help is also usually available through media representatives and their organizations, through a local college or university, or through a marketing or advertising consultant who can freelance marketing talents.

Achieving Your Goals

Your advertising message needs to relate to specific goals you may set. Chapter 18, Set Goals, will help you articulate your sales and marketing goals. Nonetheless, you will want to focus in on some of your goals as you develop your advertising message. Some advertising goals might include:

- To increase store traffic or the number of service referrals, and thereby increase sales;
- To inform target customers of a new product or service through devices such as demonstrations, free samples, ten-day home trial, two-for-one offer, sales, price rebates, or discounts;
- To build your company image, for example, an image of quality service, "We can't be undersold and we'll prove it," "We aim to please," "The bank of active people"; or
- To appeal to new target groups, such as enticing teenagers to purchase designer jeans or attracting people over 65 to join the health food and exercise clubs.

Advertising Message Summary

Your advertising message needs to inform, persuade, and remind customers that your product or service will be to their benefit — that it will satisfy their perceived needs at a fair price.

Advertising, through the wide variety of media available, is an essential ingredient of your marketing process. Your message may vary considerably depending on which media you select in your overall marketing campaign, but the basic advertisement should be designed to create customer attention, interest, desire, and action to purchase.

Step 7 of the marketing process, follow up and obtain feedback, will also be a vital part of your advertising campaign. By doing continual follow up on whether your advertising is reaching targeted customers, and getting feedback on sales effectiveness and product or service use, you can learn to master the marketing process over time. Your advertising message can be very flexible and change over time as your target customers change and your business grows.

The specific product or service, or cluster of related products or services, that you choose to advertise, and the particular image you create through advertising — in pictures, words, sounds, light, and color — can have a tremendous impact on sales. The media evaluations and comparisons of Chapter 14 will help you capitalize on this sales potential.

Worksheet 17 – Planning an Advertising Message that Supports Your Total Image

1. Write the key words, headlines, sub-headlines, and major product or service benefits you want your target customers to know about you, your product or service, or your organization in general.

   _____

   _____

   _____

   _____

   _____

2. How do you plan to organize your message so that it attracts customers' attention, interest, desire, and action?

   _____

   _____

   _____

   _____

   _____

3. Is your ad layout:

   ☐ Creative? Describe how. _____

   _____

   ☐ Unique? Describe in which ways. _____

   _____

   ☐ Specific? Does it target product, service, or groupings? Describe how. _____

   _____

   ☐ Believable? In what ways? _____

   _____

   ☐ Understandable? Describe the image created. _____

   _____

   ☐ Written with customer in mind? How? _____

   _____

   ☐ Presented with an illustration or graphic? How? How do you know it is effective? _____

   _____

Worksheet 17 – Planning an Advertising Message that Supports Your Total Image
(continued)

4. What basic information is included in the ad?

☐ Product brand name or logo   ☐ Address

☐ Telephone/800 number   ☐ Special offer deadlines

☐ Product or service guarantees   ☐ Other: _____

5. Describe how the size, length, and location of the ad are best suited to get your target market's attention.

_____

_____

_____

_____

6. Does the ad have emotional appeal? Describe how. _____

_____

_____

_____

_____

7. Does the ad have human interest appeal? Describe how. _____

_____

_____

_____

_____

8. Other ad layout factors? _____

_____

_____

_____

_____

_____

_____

_____

14 | Media Alternatives

In Chapter 13, you developed a potentially effective advertising message that caters to your target market segments and identifies the benefits of your total package of goods and services. Now you need to choose the major advertising media you will use to communicate your message. Chapter 14 discusses the major media and the advantages and disadvantages of each, including television, radio, newspapers, magazines, Yellow Pages, outdoor and indoor signs and displays, direct mail, specialty promotions, public relations, and trade shows.

In this chapter, you will find numerous worksheets and interactive question boxes to help you effectively analyze and compare all the various media. Each interactive question box provides space to note how the advertising media you just read about can benefit your product and business. Worksheet 20, Identifying Appropriate Advertising Media, at the end of this chapter provides space to identify those media you feel will be most helpful. Refer back to your answers throughout the chapter when you summarize on Worksheet 20 to make your media evaluation personal and relevant to your particular business.

Advertising Media Value Comparison

When measuring the value of various media, the standard method of comparison is to establish cost-per-thousand people exposed to the advertising message. This figure is computed the same way for any medium:

$$\text{Cost-per-Thousand (CPM)} = \frac{\text{Amount of Money Spent on Advertising}}{\text{People Exposed to Your Message}} \times 1,000$$

For example:

$$\text{CPM} = \frac{\$12,000 \text{ Ad Cost}}{2,000,000 \text{ People Exposed}} \times 1,000 = \$0.006 \text{ per person} \times 1,000$$

$$\text{CPM} = \$6.00$$

This cost per thousand value must take into consideration whether the medium reaches the target customers, or just lots of people.

A major part of budgeting your marketing campaign will be to assess, from year to year, or month to month, the cost per thousand of your chosen media. Worksheet 21, Media Evaluation and Cost Comparison, at the end of this chapter provides space to compare the relative costs and CPM of all the media discussed in this chapter. You will also find in Chapter 19 a yearly budget worksheet for assessing the CPM of your advertising media.

However, try not to choose your advertising medium solely based on cost. Instead, read through the advantages and disadvantages of the following eleven media and begin your decision making based on the usefulness of each medium to your marketing goals.

Television

Television can be a very powerful advertising medium, but it will require planning, preparation, and money to successfully harness its benefits. You need to program your advertising so that your target audience will see what you want, when you want them to see it, and with a message that grabs their attention. Television audiences tend to change channels frequently as their favorite programs come on, so advertising space is targeted to audiences that watch specific programs. You will want to obtain audience surveys from your local library and look at specific information about a particular station's audience composition at a given time. The two best known audience surveys are the *Nielsen Station Index* and the *Arbitron Index*.

For the purpose of pricing and selling television advertising, TV audiences are divided by time of day or night, and by type of program. Early morning sign-on to 4:00 P.M. is known as housespouse time; the early evening audience watches TV between 4:00 and 6:30 P.M.; prime time is 6:30 P.M. to 10:30 P.M.; and the late night fringe runs from 10:30 P.M. until sign-off. Prime time ad space is the most expensive because it has the greatest total number of viewers on any channel. However, your particular target audience may be primarily housespouses. Your advertising dollars would be more effectively spent if you purchased advertising time in the housespouse time period.

Often, just because you advertise on television — the glamour and prestige medium — you can add perceived or intangible value to your product or service. If the product or service has mass appeal, television is an excellent advertising medium to demonstrate both real and perceived benefits. If the product takes a long time to demonstrate effectively, however, a 30-second or 60-second commercial or "spot" may not be long enough, and this expensive medium may then be relatively ineffective.

Television Advantages

Television as an advertising medium can have several advantages. Consider the advantages listed here and how they apply to your product or service.

- Television is glamorous, exciting, and full of impact. It can lend these intangible qualities to your product or service.
- Television is a multisensory method of promoting your message, which can be very effective for some types of products or services.
- Visual techniques can lend an element of uniqueness to your product, and can reinforce the memory of your product in television audiences — for example, the trend toward digital imaging through advanced computer technology.
- Television can enhance your company or corporate image as part of your product's packaging.
- Television can create credibility in viewers' minds by using famous people and other believable props to promote your product or service.
- Television can enable a consumer to act immediately, when the buying impulse is strong, through a call-in phone number.
- Television can get at consumers when they are potentially least resistant, at home relaxed, and at most any hour.
- The use of TV as a retail outlet from which to buy goods may tend to make the consumer more receptive to TV commercials in advertising spots.
- Advertisers are moving toward television infomercials that seem less like advertising and more like human interest news stories about products and services.
- Interactive television and consumer promotion channels are more widespread today, and they will continue to make television an attractive advertising medium with the dawn of the information highway.

Television Advantages

Which of the advantages offered by television are most important to your overall advertising campaign, if any?

_____

_____

_____

Television Disadvantages

Television also has several disadvantages. While your product may benefit from several of the advantages television advertising offers, do not assume television advertising is the most cost-effective and beneficial form of advertising. You must weigh the pros and cons carefully. Here are some of the cons.

- Television advertising is expensive. Commercial production costs often vary from several hundred to several thousand dollars. A 30-second spot on national television could cost more than $100,000.
- TV ads can become complex, using different emphases within the same 60-second commercial, or using special effects and animation.
- Viewers can't refer back to the television message when they ultimately face the buying decision, like they can with print ads.
- Viewer receptivity can be limited, even during costly prime time, since people often leave during commercial breaks.
- The viewer may develop a bad attitude about all commercials as an interruption.

Television Disadvantages

Which potential disadvantages of television advertising would dissuade you from using it? _____

_____

_____

Does your competition use television? Why or why not? _____

_____

_____

Radio

Radio advertisements are most effective for short, repeat commercials. They are potentially less expensive than television time as measured in cost-per-thousand listeners reached (CPM). The listener tends to select one station that has a favorite type of music, a talk show, or call-in program, rather than flip channels frequently like television viewers. Radio listeners, unlike television watchers, tend to keep doing whatever they are doing during commercials, so that they are more likely to hear your advertisement many times throughout the day or week. Developing special advertising jingles and repetitive messages reinforces your message and helps potential customers recognize your product.

Most radio media strategies involve using spot ads on several stations within a local programming area to reach several target market segments. If you are developing an image to appeal to teens, working adults, and retired persons, careful selection of radio stations and a good fact sheet to the announcer can greatly help you achieve market awareness. The more spots you purchase, the less each will cost. You may want to purchase time on several stations for three months to one year to reduce costs. By submitting a fact sheet to several station announcers, your advertising message will be interpreted to suit each station's audience. This provides direct and personal appeal to your chosen market segments.

Radio Advantages

As with any advertising medium, you need to weigh the pros and cons before you settle on an ad strategy. Radio may have several advantages over television, including more intimacy and personal appeal and less expense. Read the following advantages to radio advertising with an eye to which might suit the particular advertising goals you set.

- You can target the listening audience much more specifically than with television. Local radio stations program themselves to appeal to particular groups measured by the *Nielsen* and *Arbitron Indexes*. The stations can predict the interests or buying habits of listeners to some degree so that you can target your advertising dollars effectively.

- Radio offers great flexibility. An advertising message can be pre-taped, to allow sound effects and assure professionalism, or can be read live from a fact sheet from which the announcer or disk jockey ad libs.

- Radio allows you to create an image of intimacy between your business and your target customers. When disk jockeys read from a fact sheet or ad lib, they communicate with the target audience in a personable manner — the disk jockey is a personality the listener knows. This kind of intimacy or personal interest is often not possible with television.

- Radio has a short lead time. You can take advantage of radio to advertise with little advance notice because most radio stations do not need more than 72 hours notice to broadcast a radio advertisement. Short lead time can be particularly important if your competitor starts an advertising campaign that you want to counter.

- Radio ads have a relatively low cost-per-thousand (CPM). You can keep the expense of producing a radio advertisement down by using the disk jockey's creativity — how he or she transmits your submitted radio copy — rather than spending money to produce a professional, prerecorded advertisement.

- Cost of purchasing air time is flexible — you can usually purchase time in 10-, 20-, 30-, 45- and 60-second spots. Rates are based on how many customers the radio station reaches. The most expensive radio spot ads run during the morning and evening rush hours because automobile drivers are a captive audience.

- Listeners to a particular radio station will absorb some part of an advertising message because they tend to continue activities without turning off or tuning out the advertising message.

- Radio is a medium of immediacy — the buying response is often immediate, making your ad effectiveness measurable because you can look at immediate sales increases.

Radio Advantages

What major advantages could radio advertising offer for you? _____

_____

_____

Which station(s) would be most effective in reaching potential customers? _____

_____

_____

Radio Disadvantages

Because you want to spend your advertising dollars on the ad medium with the most impact, consider carefully what advertising power you may lose via radio, particularly the power of visual imagery. Consider these disadvantages to radio advertising.

- Specific geographical targeting may be difficult, especially if the broadcast carries for many miles.

- Your ad has no visual impact as it would with television, magazines, or newspapers to help reinforce your advertising message.

- Money can be wasted when trying to reach specific target customers due to audience overlap.
- You may need to rely on the creativity of announcers to deliver your message and develop your image.

Radio Disadvantages

What major disadvantages would radio have for advertising your product or service? _____

_____

_____

Does your competition use radio? Why or why not? _____

_____

_____

Writing a Radio Commercial

If you decide to use radio advertising, the radio station staff will often help develop the message; however, you can plan ahead by using the following question format to clarify important message points. In a very short period of time, your ad copy can address:

Who? Pitch your ad to your major target market; for example, "Attention joggers." Mention your company's name as often as possible. Repetition is good to reinforce memory, and if someone tunes in late, physically or mentally, some part of the ad may catch the listener's ear well into the commercial.

What? What is the product or service niche? What benefits does the product provide? Tell your listeners what the product or service will do for them; for example, "Remove stains without scrubbing."

Where? Identify the location of the business; help the listeners find the product or service. Use action words; for example, "Get to Mike's at the corner of 5th and Main — take Main one block north of the Municipal Stadium."

When? When is your product available? For how long? Beginning when?

Why? Why should consumers buy your product now? Can you give your listeners any additional enticement to act now rather than later; for example, "Today only — Joe Johnson will autograph free pictures of his last winning game."

How? How can the listener get, buy, or find your product easily? For example, you can include a telephone number and encourage listeners to, "Call this number right now."

With the help of the guidelines outlined above and Worksheet 18, Radio Copy Format, at the end of this chapter, write a radio commercial for your product. Read it aloud. Is it easily understood? How long does it take to read? Would you want the disc jockey to read your fact sheet? Once you have developed a sample ad, you will know better how effective radio advertising can be for your business.

Newspapers

More money is spent in newspaper advertising each year than in any other medium. In general, newspapers contain local advertising. Local newspaper ads offer you greater selectivity in reaching your target market than either television or radio ads, and they work well to fill readers' needs and expectations — newspaper readers often turn to newspaper ads specifically to find certain types of local advertising. Classified advertising is suited to target a readership that is ready, willing, and able to purchase right away. Out of every ten classified shoppers who buy, two are impulse buyers and eight have definitely planned to buy the kind of item they purchased.

Space devoted to display advertising is usually a large part of the total advertising space in the paper. As a rule of thumb, the larger the display ad, the greater the sales impact. Your ad may be more effective if placed as one large display ad in the Sunday paper rather than as small space ads every other day during the week. Trial and error and observing the space buying habits of your competitors will give you an idea of what will work best for your business.

Newspaper advertising space is usually purchased by the dimensions of depth (the number of lines) and width (the number of columns). As an industry standard, 14 agate lines make up a column inch, no matter how wide the column is.

For example, assume you want to buy display space that is two columns wide and six inches deep. This ad would amount to a space that is 12 column inches (2 x 6). To determine the number of agate lines, multiply the number of column inches by 14. If the cost of the advertisement is $1.00 per agate line, display advertising in the preceding example would cost $168.00 (12 column inches x 14 agate lines/inch x $1.00 per agate line).

The cost of display advertising may be affected by other pricing policies of the newspaper's publisher. Policies vary, but they are usually affected by competition from other newspapers. Newspapers usually sell a total amount of space during a year based on a contract or multiple insertion basis. In addition, prices change due to the amount and nature of the newspaper's readership. Neighborhood shopping gazettes offer cheaper rates than do big city newspapers, though they may be more effective in reaching target customers. Most newspapers have circulations that are daily, weekly, or Sunday, and all offer a great opportunity to expand sales through advertising.

You can enjoy valuable customer targeting by placing your ad in special reader sections, such as sports, business, features, or women's pages. For example, if you are selling executive calendars, the best place for your ad may be the business section, whereas the introduction of a new basketball shoe may get better results in the sports section. Customers may also expect to find certain products or services in certain sections.

You can use newspaper readers' habits to your advantage. Readers tend to turn first to the section that interests them most. This presents an opportunity for your ad to catch their eye in relation to the editorial content they enjoy. Newspapers have the distinct advantage of being able to provide greater detail over longer periods of time than any other advertising medium, with the possible exception of magazines.

Today, most people rely on their local newspaper for local and regional news. People enjoy reading about their locality and about the people they know. Many readers look forward to the weekend shopping specials and rely on the newspaper to introduce new retail products and service outlets.

Because of their local nature, newspapers are very effective in creating awareness of a location. Consumers often use newspaper ads to do their comparison shopping. Automobile dealerships, major retail outlets, real estate agencies, and supermarkets rely heavily on the newspaper because their readership is more limited — ideal for attracting local customers to a new local business. It is important to calculate the cost of advertising per 1,000 readers reached (CPM) by the newspaper to determine the most effective use of your advertising dollar.

Newspaper Advantages

If your target market is local, newspaper advertising may be the most effective medium for you. Read the following advantages to newspaper advertising to find out if it is most conducive to your advertising goals.

- Almost every geographic location in the United States has at least one local newspaper that can quickly respond to your advertising needs.

- Materials given for ad insertion usually take less lead time than for other media.

- Readers look forward to browsing through their newspaper and have become habituated to using display and classified advertising to help do their comparative shopping.

- The quick response to a sales message can help deplete unwanted inventories or introduce new products and services.

- The selectivity of neighborhood papers offers a low-cost opportunity to try different ad copy aimed at different audiences to test various advertising approaches.

- Newspapers offer a less intrusive advertising forum than either television or radio and people can refer back to specific ads.

- Newspaper ads have great flexibility in placement and timing that allows you the time to respond to your competition and to changing market conditions.

- Newspapers allow the greatest opportunity to reduce expenses through cooperative advertising allowances from manufacturers.

Newspaper Advantages

How would newspaper advertising be especially advantageous to you? _____

_____

_____

What are the most appropriate newspapers? _____

_____

_____

Newspaper Disadvantages

While newspaper advertising may be fast and flexible, it does have some drawbacks relative to other forms of advertising. You cannot include color or sound in your ad, elements that may be important to advertising your product. Consider how your advertising goals may be affected by newspaper disadvantages.

- Newspapers suffer from the same clutter problems as do other media. Unless an ad is creative and stands out from others, it may not reach a particular target market effectively.

- If the reader is in a hurry, the editorial content may attract most attention at the expense of the advertising page.
- Most newspaper ads are black and white, eliminating the ability to attract interest if the product is colorful.
- Newsprint is porous and doesn't permit some ads to reproduce well.

Newspaper Disadvantages

What are some of the disadvantages that newspaper advertising might have for you? _____

_____

_____

Does your competition use newspaper advertising? Why or why not? _____

_____

_____

Magazines

One of the greatest benefits of magazine advertising is that you can use full-color displays and special effects. Like other print media, magazines rely on visual impact; therefore, you must conceptualize your sales approach for magazine ads to take advantage of that visual impact. Since magazines are now produced to appeal to geographic regions or specific interest groups, small businesses can effectively promote a product or service, usually at a lower cost than with television or daily newspapers.

Advertising in a national magazine has the same prestige as national television advertising. People assume that advertisers in national publications have reliable and high-quality products and services. You can achieve the prestige of a national publication, but keep the cost and exposure to a regional basis by using regional editions available from many national magazines.

The opportunities for using magazine ads are increasing because magazines are becoming more specialized and publishing regional editions. Catering to special interest groups, such as teens, business owners, retired people, homeowners, and women, and special fields of interest, such as show business, computers, sports, cooking, travel, and gardening, is now the norm for magazine publishers. For example, more than 50 publications cater to users of small computers, and another 20 magazines are devoted to home-based businesses. This trend offers marketers greater precision in reaching the special interest groups that would most likely buy their offerings.

If you want to reach people who manage rubbish disposal and supply equipment of that industry, *Solid Waste* magazine might be appropriate. If you want to reach automobile builders, dealers, or associated prospects, possibly *Automotive Age* is the answer. If your message is geared to super-market personnel, *Progressive Grocer* could be your key to reaching your target market. Do you want to address the quick-stop mini market outlets? Try *Convenience Store News*. Magazine advertising has tremendous potential for target advertising.

Magazine Advantages

You may overcome some of the disadvantages of other print media, such as newspapers, by using magazine ads, which permit you to use large color displays to evoke vivid images of your product and its benefits. Consider the following advantages to using magazine ads.

- Since magazines are normally kept around the house or office for many months, they are likely to be passed along to many other readers who don't necessarily buy the magazine.
- Magazines are often reread many times by potential customers who may take time to reach a buying decision and can be positively reinforced to buy each time they see the advertisement.
- You can easily research advertising costs and media contacts at the public library in the Standard Rate and Data Service (SRDS) magazine directory.
- Magazines can provide vivid color displays and special creative effects like holography that support a visual image in the reader's mind.

Magazine Advantages

What specific advantages could magazine advertising provide for you? _____

_____

_____

Which local and national magazines might be appropriate for advertising your product or service? _____

_____

_____

Magazine Disadvantages

While you can accomplish several marketing goals with a magazine ad, such as national exposure of your product, you may lose some dollar effectiveness due to long lead times and difficult-to-quantify results of magazine display ads. Consider the following disadvantages to magazine advertising.

- The planning required for insertion of display advertisements requires two or more months lead time.

- Since many magazines are published monthly or quarterly, the opportunity for rapid response or follow-up advertising is limited.

- Since many people read more than one magazine in their field of interest, advertising in several magazines may duplicate circulation coverage, thereby reducing dollar effectiveness and increasing cost per thousand exposed.

- Magazines are more effective in promoting overall marketing image than for special purposes, such as sales.

Magazine Disadvantages

What disadvantages, if any, do you see in advertising your product or service in magazines? _____

_____

_____

Does your competition use magazine advertising? Why or why not? _____

_____

_____

Yellow Pages and Business Service Directories

Every American community has its phone book, and many communities often have other business directories. For many small businesses, the major form of advertising is the telephone book. Beauty salons, barbershops, plumbers, air conditioning or other appliance repair businesses, and restaurants all rely heavily on the Yellow Pages for customers. Since the Yellow Pages are published only once a year, listing your business under more than one category, although more expensive, is often an effective advertising strategy and is highly recommended, especially if you work out of your home. There is also a growing trend for newsprint service directories, like *Common Ground*, that cover advertising and listings for nontraditional specialized services.

Directory Advantages

Yellow Page advertising is the primary form of advertising for many small businesses because it can be very effective in cost per thousand readers reached. Consider, for example, these important advantages to Yellow Page advertising.

- Every home and business has a telephone book.
- Most people are conditioned to use the Yellow Page listing for locating the product or service they need.

Directory Advantages

How would advertising in the Yellow Pages or local business directory be beneficial to your business? _____

_____

_____

What categories would you list under? _____

_____

_____

Directory Disadvantages

Despite the extensive exposure you can get from directory advertising, advertising through the Yellow Pages and other directories does have several disadvantages. Consider carefully how you should combine Yellow Page ads with other advertising media. You will need to pay particular attention to these disadvantages.

- Planning is necessary to include display advertising before the deadline. Opening a new business cannot necessarily be timed to the publishing of the Yellow Pages.
- Telephones for the business must be connected and paid for many months before the Yellow Pages publication.

- Consumers may not know the product is available or what listing it would be under. What listings would you look under to find worms for your garden, for instance?

- It may be too much to spend for a small business, especially one whose target market is very small and highly localized.

Directory Disadvantages

How might your advertising goals suffer by using the Yellow Pages or other directories as your primary advertising medium? _____

_____

_____

Does your competition use Yellow Pages advertising? Why or why not?

_____

_____

Outdoor Signs and Displays

Everyone is accustomed to reading signs wherever they go — indoors and outside. Signs of all sorts help identify your image in a potential customer's mind. Outdoor signs work for you around the clock, attracting the attention of anyone who passes by and sees the sign. Signs and displays create impressions, awareness, reminders that your business is available to fill customers' needs. Customers rely on signs and displays to help locate a business or product within a business location, mall, or downtown shopping area.

Unlike billboards, signage outside your storefront or office will help customers find your business, even if it is on the 15th floor. For manufacturing, wholesale, or retail outlets, a storefront sign is often the first image passersby see. The sign's impression should be positive, identifiable, and associated with the product you offer. You can take advantage of the fleeting moment when passersby see your sign by using neon, special lighting, or lettering effects to attract their attention.

Other forms of outdoor advertising include transit posters on buses — both inside and outside the bus — and on taxis, commuter trains and subways, and transit station walls. You can make poster displays very creative and colorful, and they reproduce well, which helps maintain the image of high quality you want your advertising to project about your product. Poster displays are relatively inexpensive considering the daily commuters who become a captive audience for the poster's advertising message.

Outdoor Sign Advantages

Signs, poster displays, and billboards can be extremely effective advertising media for promoting awareness of various products and services that appeal to a mass market, since cost per thousand viewers is very reasonable. Consider these other advantages to outdoor signs and displays.

- Physically, outdoor signs are the largest form of advertising available, which may truly impress potential customers.
- Storefront and office signage are essential to helping interested customers locate and remember you.
- Signs and displays support and reinforce other forms of advertising that are part of your current marketing strategy.
- You can use color reproduction, illumination, and spectacular special effects, especially on large, well-located billboards, to create a unique and lasting image of your product and your business.

Outdoor Sign Advantages

Is your office or store easy to find?   Yes ☐ No ☐

Is any additional signage needed to help find your business or help advertise it?   Yes ☐ No ☐

Would billboard advertising be effective for your product?   Yes ☐ No ☐

Describe the ideal signage for your place of business. _____

_____

_____

Outdoor Sign Disadvantages

Almost every form of advertising requires special consideration and expertise to produce the desired results. Signs, displays, and billboards may require more planning and care than you might first imagine. Consider the following issues carefully before you include this advertising medium as part of your marketing plan.

- Billboards should be located in high traffic areas to be effective. You may have to wait for access to display your signs in high demand areas.

- Billboards and signage must be unobstructed and tilted correctly on the traffic side of the road to be effective.

- Transit advertising is easily vandalized.

- Billboards must be attention-getting, succinct, and bold.

- Signage is often highly regulated — in some areas, storefront signage is limited in size and visibility by local ordinance.

- Billboards and other forms of outdoor advertising may be seen as polluting the environment, thereby giving a negative association with your product to some groups or individuals. Many metropolitan areas and counties have greatly reduced or eliminated billboard advertising as part of their political consciousness.

Outdoor Sign Disadvantages

Are there any legal restrictions on the types of signs you can have outside your business?   Yes ☐ No ☐

Does your competition use outdoor signs, displays, or billboard advertising? Why or why not? _____

_____

_____

Indoor Signs and Displays

Indoor signs have the same basic purpose as outdoor ones — to provide information about your product and service offerings and their location. Point-of-purchase displays, unless they involve special expensive production techniques, are an extremely cost-effective means not only of creating awareness of your product or service, but also of enticing customers to purchase immediately. You do not need to schedule advertising in advance.

In a local neighborhood store, window signs and displays can create awareness in passersby and are very effectively used by small business owners as a means of promoting new products or services, sales, or end-of-season closeouts. You can also use window displays to create a store atmosphere that is inviting — for example, holiday window displays at Halloween, Thanksgiving, and Christmas. Window displays offer you a way of visually promoting many products at a time, thereby increasing effective use of selling space. You can change displays frequently. Customers often ask for a product "just like the one in the window."

You can effectively tie point-of-purchase displays to your current advertising in your local newspaper or radio station; for example, your television ad might say, "Look for the happy clown display at our store." A good display directs customers drawn in by advertising to the product and reinforces their intention to buy.

The best use of point-of-purchase displays is to place the display in a high traffic area at a height at which customers can clearly identify it — often on the counter, in the entrance way, or at the cash register. Design your point-of-purchase displays to encourage customers to speed up their buying decision — to make the purchase now rather than later.

Indoor Sign Advantages

One of the major advantages to using indoor signage is how well it complements other types of advertising media. Consider these advantages to window, point-of-purchase, and other indoor signs as you build your marketing plan.

- In-house signs and point-of-purchase displays are an inexpensive way of supporting correlated media advertisements.
- You can use indoor signs to promote sale items not advertised concurrently in other media.
- Every shopkeeper and service outlet can use interior signage.
- Window displays and point-of-purchase displays are extremely flexible because you can change them as often as you need.
- Signs can serve as a kind of road map within your shop or office to inform and attract customers and invite them to try a sample of the product as a purchase incentive.

Indoor Sign Advantages

Describe how indoor signs or displays can be used to the best advantage for your business. _____

_____

_____

_____

Indoor Sign Disadvantages

Indoor signs need some special consideration as an advertising tool. Consider the following special concerns and how they may affect how you use indoor signs and point-of-purchase displays.

- Displays need to be interesting, exciting, creative, and informative without cluttering the window or counter.

- The manufacturer or wholesaler cannot be assured that the point-of-purchase display will be kept in good shape or located in a high traffic area. Many good displays end up under the counter, in the trash can, or behind some obstacle, unused.

- The displays are not always timely — the sign needs changing the day after a special event. For example, after Valentine's Day, the candy display keeps advertising even if all items are gone.

Indoor Sign Disadvantages

What disadvantages might you suffer from using indoor signs and point-of-purchase displays? How can you overcome them? _____

_____

_____

Does your competition utilize indoor signs and displays effectively? Why or why not? _____

_____

_____

Direct Mail

Many types direct mail advertisements are used to great success by small businesses. The message presented on a flyer or brochure may describe your business, explain an expensive or complicated new product, give detailed benefits of your service, provide technical specification — whatever information cannot fit in a mass-media ad.

You can also offer certain things not usually advertised in other media, such as household hints, consumer awareness blurbs, recipes, sports tips, and coupons for free trial offers, through flyers and announcements. Flyers and brochures are more likely to remain in prospective buyers' possession until they need what you offer. You can also hand out flyers inexpensively rather than mail them.

One of the major reasons businesspeople like direct-mail advertising is that they can target their message to specific groups by purchasing mailing lists. As long as the lists are kept up to date, you will probably reach your target markets. You can also rent mailing lists from mail list services who maintain and update them. For most businesses, the best mailing list is of their current customers. Use receipts, customer logs, and sign-up sheets to keep track of your customers over the years and develop your marketing database.

Service businesses can use flyers to announce their existence at a low cost to a very specific target audience, for instance, the new tax service in the shopping center. You can mail an informational brochure about your local community service and the recipient can file it away knowing they have a familiar and local contact when they are ready to purchase the needed service.

Although direct-mail is the most expensive in cost per thousand, it can be the most effective means of advertising because of the unusually high response rate this medium can elicit. By controlling the time of mailing, the mailing list, the product offerings, pricing, and benefits, you can discover what works best to promote a particular product or service, especially a new one.

Direct-mail catalogs are a type of business all their own — essentially a business or organization in a book, distributed door-to-door or through the mail. Since catalogs are used as reference books, both home and business users tend to keep them on the shelf. Catalogs are valuable in retail outlets, wholesale businesses, which may develop their own product catalogs, and manufacturers who produce a line of products and use catalogs to create awareness of their product prices, specifications, and warranties, such as The Sharper Image.

Organizations that rely heavily on catalogs and direct mail for their business often spend 50% or more of their total annual sales on direct-mail campaigns. The expense can be enormous, but so can the profits. For many businesses, mail order is their business — an entire way of life, often started out of a home initially. In fact, estimates are that up to 20% of all advertising dollars are spent on direct-mail advertising — more than $1.1 billion annually. The annual Publishers Clearing House, *Reader's Digest*, and other major direct-mail campaigns attempt to reach every household in the country with prizes and contests as incentives to purchase their product offerings. If you are interested in starting your own mail order business and want to know more about the legal and cost implications, consult The Oasis Press' *Mail Order Legal Guide.*

Direct Mail Advantages

Direct mail offers some very unique advantages. Consider how the following advantages to direct-mail advertising may contribute to your overall marketing goals.

- Direct mail advertising offers the benefit of being more measurable than any other major medium. When people order from the catalog or send in a mailed out coupon, you know your ad is working.
- Direct mail offers a high degree of flexibility — you can produce flyers and brochures in any size, color, and shape.
- You can use direct mail to test the same basic ad with different ad copy or design to see what pulls the best response.
- With computerized mailing list programs, a home-based business can keep its expenses down. You can also buy mailing lists on floppy disc to expand your own customer base.
- Consumers are aware that mail-order companies have low company overhead. They, therefore, often associate mail-order catalogs and direct-mail flyers and coupon envelopes with bargain values. You can use this public perception to your advantage if you use direct-mail advertising.
- Many people respond to the excitement of a percentage discount — 10% quantity discount or 50% discount if you purchase by a certain date, for example. Direct mail is well suited to advertising discounts and free trial offers.
- Direct mail is a highly selective medium because you can decide who will receive your mailer by renting highly selective mailing lists or selectively distributing handbills to desirable target customers.
- You can mail your direct-mail advertising at any time, without the hassle of planning ahead for copy deadlines, as required with other media.

Direct Mail Advantages

Describe a direct-mail campaign that would be effective for your firm.

_____

_____

How would you get a mailing list? _____

_____

_____

What is the cost? _____

Direct Mail Disadvantages

If even 2% of the people who get your mailer purchase your product or service, you may consider your campaign a success. However, achieving that 2% can be difficult. Consider some of these potential problems to a direct-mail advertising campaign.

- From the moment the mail arrives or the flyer is distributed, it may have the undivided attention of a potential customer. However, direct-mail advertisements need to be catchy and informative enough to maintain the customer's attention long enough to respond — or they can easily end up in the wastepaper basket.

- Unless the mailing list is both up to date and reliable in terms of its categorization (age, sex, profession, lifestyle characteristics, etc.), money is wasted. Up to 25% of most lists require an address change within a given year.

- Someone must manage the mailing, which involves stuffing envelopes, handling the postage, and sorting for a bulk mailing. You can overcome this hassle by hiring a distribution or postering service, but that is an additional expense.

Direct Mail Disadvantages

What disadvantages might a direct-mail campaign have for your particular product or service? _____

_____

_____

Does your competition utilize direct mail? Why or why not? _____

_____

_____

Special Promotions and Specialty Advertising

Special promotional advertising can take many different forms. Companies use calendars, pens, pencils, balloons, key chains, T-shirts, visors, and hats as special promotional items — almost anything you can imprint with your company name or logo and pass out to potential customers will help support other advertising efforts. Customers often enjoy receiving and using these "freebies" just for that reason — everyone feels good about receiving something useful for free.

This promotional medium is flexible and often very inexpensive, especially if you choose low-cost items to give away. If you take advantage of quantity discounts when you purchase the item you will give away, you can keep the expense of this type of advertising very low. Include as part of the promotional item your company name, phone number, and address, and perhaps a catchy motto or phrase that your target customers will remember as part of your business' unique image.

For example, one midwestern manufacturer of precision tube-bending equipment gave out a good quality ballpoint pen inscribed with the company name, logo, and motto: "We bend to please." It was frequently referred to by customers as a useful item that they enjoyed receiving with each sales order. Pens tend to get left on tables and passed along — which is very helpful in spreading your message and contributing to your overall marketing strategy.

Other special promotions include special incentives to entice manufacturers and retailers to promote the product. These might include special coupons, trading stamps, two-for-one offers, manufacturer's rebate, contests among sales personnel, cash bonuses and awards, free vacations, special offers on related products and services, volume and frequency of purchase discounts — and many other possibilities. Creative merchandisers talk to others in their channels of distribution to share new ideas and agree to use cooperative advertising arrangements that have worked in the past. Local shopping centers often develop their own coupon ad booklets with specials to attract new customers and promote sales to existing clientele.

Another type of promotional offer is aimed more at your sales force than at your customers. You can offer a trip for two to Jamaica to the top salesperson of the month. This type of sales promotion package not only serves as a morale booster for people who help promote your product or service, but it can also dramatically increase your sales.

You can also target groups who might purchase your product in bulk with a promotional package. You can offer special discounts to youth groups or senior citizens for them to buy your product or your service — especially helpful if they are slow making their buying decision or if they are being targeted by your competition with a similar advertising strategy.

Special in-store promotions should, of course, be supported through other media such as storefront banners, point-of-purchase displays and demonstrations, promotional literature or handouts, floor displays, or shopping bags, especially for holidays. These kinds of special promotions should have a beginning and an end so that they create excitement with other people in your distribution channels, sales personnel, and potential customers.

Special Promotion Advantages

A special promotion campaign can help you distinguish yourself in the marketplace or highlight the introduction of a new product or a special event at relatively little expense. Consider the following advantages to specialty advertising.

- Special sales promotions allow you a great deal of variety at the product distribution level, retail level, and consumer level.
- Whatever is offered as a sales incentive to the distributor, retailer, or customer involves a relatively small expense for the extra dollars brought into your organization.
- Special promotions can help shape your total image in the marketplace by creating excitement, incentive, and distinction in the eyes of your distributors, sales personnel, and potential customers.

Special Promotion Advantages

List some specialty promotion ideas that would help sell your product or service. _____

_____

_____

_____

Special Promotion Disadvantages

Specialty advertising requires a certain degree of planning and timing to have a maximum effect. Pay particular attention to the following potential disadvantages to specialty advertising:

- Special sales promotions should relate your product or service offerings to the total image you want to create.
- Special promotions need to be well-timed in relation to your other advertising efforts — watch the effective date of coupon discount expiration.
- Special promotions may only attract those who take advantage of free offers or discounts but never intend to be a customer.

Special Promotion Disadvantages

What disadvantages does specialty advertising hold for your product? _____

_____

_____

Does your competition utilize specialty advertising? If so, how? _____

_____

_____

Public Relations and Publicity

Good public and community relations require you to project the particular image you want to achieve in the marketplace. Public relations (PR) is usually a free or inexpensive way for a small business owner to get his or her name, product or service, or business event into public awareness. Successful PR helps to create recognition of your business or of various new or positive aspects of your product or service mix. Joining organizations like Rotary, Toastmasters, or business and professional associations, creating a memorable grand opening for a new retail outlet, or announcing tours through your manufacturing plant help support your company image and spread news about your business through community contact.

The ways in which you can create good public relations vary with your location and the local media available. You can join fraternal organizations, community involvement groups, and networking business lunch or dinner groups. This trend is rapidly growing as home-based business owners network with each other in ever-widening business communities. You can invite media personalities to hear you speak at the local community college, attend a lecture, see a slide presentation at the community center — anything you are involved in can help give your business exposure through positive publicity and community involvement.

You can often develop public relations and good publicity around a unique community event, new office, employee, or promotion. You can build the story, or press release, around just about any product or service aspect, as long as it is timely or newsworthy. For example, if you can get a local newspaper to pick up on a press release you send out, a headline like "Veterinarian Makes House Calls," can generate a great amount of free publicity for your pet clinic. Remember, the newsworthy story or event must be true in order to maintain your integrity and build customer trust and loyalty.

Public Relations Advantages

PR is a good way to build name recognition for your product and business as long as the publicity is consistent with your image. Consider the following advantages to using PR as part of your advertising campaign.

- Publicity in the news media is free to those who can create enough interest or newsworthiness to obtain an interview or writeup.
- The newsworthy nature of the product or service can be developed into a column for a newspaper or magazine.
- You can use public relations and publicity to shape your total image.

Public Relations Advantages

List the organizations and associations to which you currently belong or should consider joining. _____

_____

_____

Identify a newsworthy item about your business, and then write a brief publicity statement about yourself, your organization, or some unique aspects of the products or services. _____

_____

_____

_____

Public Relations Disadvantages

PR can be an inexpensive and effective way to build name and product recognition in the marketplace, but it can also backfire. Consider the following potential dangers as you prepare your public relations campaign.

- The media can interpret publicity generated by a special event, such as an open house or a speech, according to the writer's viewpoint — which isn't always what you had in mind.

- The cost of hiring a public relations firm or agent can vary greatly in cost, and the effects of good public relations and publicity are difficult to measure.

Public Relations Disadvantages

How will you measure the success of a PR campaign? _____

_____

_____

Do your competitors use PR or publicity in their marketing efforts? To which organizations or associations do your competitors belong? _____

_____

_____

Writing a Press Release

One of the best ways to generate publicity for your newsworthy item is to write a press release. You can write the press release yourself, or hire a PR agency to write it for you. Then send it directly to various media representatives, local radio and television stations, and newspapers.

When you write a press release, follow these important guidelines.

- Whom to contact for more information should be the first item at the top of the page. Include the name, address, and telephone number.

- Include the release date at the top — usually "For Immediate Release."

- Give your press release a headline — a short descriptive summary of what is in the press release in four to twelve factual words.

- In the body of the press release, give details in the first paragraph of where, why, and when the news event is taking place and who or what is involved. Keep it short and simple. A few additional paragraphs may add less important details. Include information on what readers should do if interested, such as buy tickets, order tapes, reserve space, or secure catalogs.

- Type the press release and double-space — one to two pages at most. Send an original or a good photocopy.

- Determine where to send the press release. If the news item is of interest to people who fish, maybe a fishing magazine would be appropriate, or maybe your local paper or radio or television station. Is the event something the publication or program usually covers? Are you after professional or trade reputation or an increase in customers? Who are your customers? What media do they watch, read, or listen to?

- Identify the name of a specific person to receive your press release. Magazines and periodicals list specific editors of different sections, for example, the lifestyles, business, sports, around the town, or education sections. Call the radio and television stations to determine the name of a current publicity or public relations person. Your local business library may have directories, such as Ayres and Standard Rate and Data Service (SRDS), that may have printed the local contact person or can give you a number to call to help you locate that person, usually updated annually.

- Follow up. Call after a week to determine if the material was received and can be used. If it isn't being used, determine why not or when it will be used.

- Be prepared for an interview, either with someone from your organization or with satisfied customers who might be willing to have their names used as examples of past successes.

As you begin your publicity campaign, you might want to keep a database of press contacts for sending press releases or other announcements. For a more specific example of how to write a press release, see the sample on page 171, at the end of this chapter. Worksheet 19, Write Your Own Press Release, on page 172 will also lead you step-by-step through the process of writing a press release.

Trade Shows, Fairs, Professional Meetings

Trade shows, fairs, or large gatherings of similar types of businesses or services offer real potential for seeing the latest fashions or newest ideas — for example, in computer hardware or software at COMDEC in Las Vegas every year — and being seen by those most interested in finding out about you and your product or service. Buyers and sellers have an opportunity in a concentrated time and space to see what is available. Professional organizers lease or rent a facility and usually plan the promotion. They rent out booth or display spaces.

Many businesses successfully use trade show demonstrations to attract customers. For example, a software game designer had no idea how to market his product. He was able to demonstrate the game at a computer trade show where a major computer producer expressed an interest — a computer company that had told him over the telephone that they were not interested. The game designer posted sign-up sheets for interested attendees to get their name on a mailing list. By the end of the trade show, the game designer had begun to build a database of potential customers that he would now target with direct mail flyers to try his new software free for a limited time.

Trade Show Advantages

Trade shows, fairs, and industry conferences allow you to have face-to-face contact with potential customers, distributors, suppliers, and, of course, competitors. This kind of contact provides excellent opportunities for networking, learning, and marketing. Consider some of these advantages to attending trade shows and demonstrations.

- Most people attending shows are there to find out about the products or services being displayed.
- It provides an excellent opportunity to demonstrate a product to interested people.
- Product displays remain set up throughout the show to maximize product exposure, whether or not you are in your booth.
- You can see what the competition is offering.
- Names can be collected to add to a mailing list.
- It is a good opportunity to get consumer feedback and product improvement ideas.
- Opportunity to find new distributors for your product or service.

Trade Show Advantages

What trade shows, seminars, fairs, demonstrations, or meetings might be beneficial to attend? _____

_____

_____

What are the major advantages of attending one of these shows or seminars?

_____

_____

_____

Trade Show Disadvantages

Sometimes, a great gathering of people in your industry does not translate into great sales. You need to research a trade show carefully before you spend the time and money to prepare for it. Find out who organizes the meeting. Consider these potential disadvantages.

- Competitors can see what you are offering.
- It may attract a lot of just lookers, not prospective buyers, depending on how well the occasion was advertised.
- Organizers may be more interested in selling space than getting the kind of people to attend the event in the numbers that will produce the best results.
- Customers may want to bargain or negotiate more with many choices available.

Trade Show Disadvantages

How will you measure the results of trade show marketing and networking?

_____

_____

_____

What shows do your major competitors attend? _____

_____

_____

_____

Media Alternatives Summary

Please note that although some of the media alternatives discussed in this chapter are obviously more expensive than others, and some have a longer list of identifiable advantages and disadvantages, none is necessarily more important than another in your overall marketing strategy. You may have to determine over time and use which media combinations are most effective for creating awareness of your product or service among your target customers. Customer follow up and feedback, Step 7 of the marketing process, allows you to determine which media will work best for you.

➪ The Evergreen Indoor Plant Nursery has developed an advertising campaign its owners believe will create customer awareness of its products and services. Paul and Ellen plan to use five primary advertising media in combination to maximize cost-effectiveness. The advertising media include:

- Direct Mail — Develop a brochure, in cooperation with their main supplier, to use as a direct-mail piece; the brochure can also be used in point-of-purchase displays;

- Public Relations — Send out a press release about plant containers produced by a local artisan; write an article for a local business paper on the benefit of plants on air quality in closed offices;

- Specialty Advertising — Sponsor a contest for local businesses who care about air quality in their offices, with a prize of $500 worth of plants and a free consultation;

- Yellow Pages — Place ads under both "interior decorating" and "plant nurseries;" and

- Trade Show — Develop a display for a local office products trade show.

Paul and Ellen will also try to create awareness among local businesses by leaving a small, complimentary plant at several office buildings nearby, along with a brochure and a note that reads, "Compliments of Evergreen Indoor Plant Nursery — the nursery that cares for your air."

Once you have a good idea of major advertising media and their advantages, as the Evergreen Indoor Plant Nursery has in this example, you can use Worksheet 20, Identifying Appropriate Advertising Media, at the end of this chapter to summarize your planned advertising approach. Use the notes you have taken throughout this chapter to assist you. Worksheet 21, Media Evaluation and Cost Comparison, then leads you through a cost comparison of the various media discussed in this chapter. This cost comparison will be important when you develop your marketing budget in Chapter 19.

Worksheet 18 – Radio Copy Format

In the space below, fill in the blanks with the phrases, jingles, and words you want a radio announcer to use in delivering your message. This ad copy can then be sent to your chosen radio stations for commercial delivery. Also, try reading the ad first yourself to estimate the air time you will need to purchase.

Company name: _____

Contact: _____

Product/Service description: _____

_____

Address: _____ Telephone number: _____

_____

Target audience: _____

_____

_____

Copy content — major points to be covered — who, what, where, when, why, how:

_____

_____

_____

_____

_____

_____

_____

Any special instructions to the radio announcer:

_____

_____

_____

_____

_____

_____

_____

_____

_____

Sample Press Release

Contact: Mike Harrigan   FOR IMMEDIATE RELEASE

Out of State College Advisors
6832 Rozak Street
Dallas, Texas 75081
(214) 697-0048

COUNSELING FOR COLLEGE BOUND GETS VISUAL AID

Dallas - Mike Harrigan is Texas' first freelance college counselor with an additional first. A former admissions officer at Harvard, Harrigan and two colleagues run Out of State College Advisors, a private service which provides, in addition to current information, video shorts showing campus life on over 100 campuses in the United States.

"My purpose is to give the eager college-bound student visual information about other colleges and universities. The student can sit in on classes, visit dorms, see professors, all in one central facility," says Harrigan. "High school counselors try to inform students of opportunities. I just have the visual resources and the time to work one-on-one to match up the students' abilities, needs and wants with what is available."

The counseling session includes discussion of test scores, grade points, extracurricular activities and career planning issues. Decisions can then be made about what is the best combination of an affordable and desirable college. The fee structures are based on the extent of counseling desired. For more information call Mike Harrigan at (214) 697-0048.

Worksheet 19 – Write Your Own Press Release

FOR IMMEDIATE RELEASE

Contact: _____

Organization: _____

Address: _____

Phone number: _____

Heading: _____

Body:

_____

_____

_____

_____

_____

_____

Action reader is asked to take: _____

_____

List newspapers, radio and TV stations, magazines, and periodicals to send your press release to and identify the main contact person at each source.

_____

_____

_____

_____

_____

_____

This press release will be mailed on: _____

Follow-up phone calls will be made on: _____

Preparation for follow-up interviews include: _____

_____

Worksheet 20 – Identifying Appropriate Advertising Media

Check the forms of media that seem most advantageous for your business. Identify which particular benefits these major media have for you and how often you would like to use them. Also, identify which media your competitors use in the space provided.

Good for Your Business	Used by Your Competitors	
☐	☐	Television: Which channels? Which frequencies?
☐	☐	Radio: Which stations? Which frequencies?
☐	☐	Newspapers: Which ones? Which sections?
☐	☐	Magazines: Which ones? Which sections? Which editions?
☐	☐	Yellow Pages: Which section listings? Which other business service directories?
☐	☐	Printed promotional materials and direct mail?
☐	☐	Outdoor signs and displays?
☐	☐	Indoor signs and displays?
☐	☐	Trade shows and fairs?

Worksheet 20 – Identifying Appropriate Advertising Media (continued)

Check which types of promotional materials, signs, displays, or publicity events you would like to use in your advertising campaign.

☐ Letterheads/envelopes

☐ Flyers/brochures

☐ Business forms

☐ Informational pamphlets

☐ Catalogs

☐ Special announcements

☐ Seasonal sales

☐ Grand openings

☐ Product specification sheets

☐ Market research questionnaires

☐ Billboards

☐ Reader boards

☐ Point-of-purchase displays

☐ Product demonstrations

☐ Bus and transit advertising

☐ Special clearance sales

☐ Awards and prizes

☐ Contests

☐ Parades

☐ Press releases

☐ Press conferences

☐ Interviews (radio and television)

☐ Invitations

☐ Appointment cards

☐ Coupons

☐ Gift certificates

☐ Thank-you notes/cards

☐ Registration forms

☐ Newsletters

☐ Evaluation forms

☐ Special one-time-only offers

☐ Direct-mail materials (mailing lists)

☐ Floor displays

☐ Exhibits/trade show displays

☐ Posters

☐ In-house product information

☐ Arts and crafts festivals

☐ In-house product information racks

☐ Open houses

☐ Sidewalk sales

☐ Grand openings

☐ Business or personal profiles

☐ Feature articles

☐ Photographs

Worksheet 21 – Media Evaluation and Cost Comparison

Research your library and make phone calls to fill in this worksheet. Careful research will help you compare the various advertising media and their relative costs. Refer also to Worksheet 20, where you assessed the appropriateness of particular media for your advertising campaign.

Media	Circulation	Audience Type	Cost per ad	Cost per 1,000	Frequency of ad	Expected Response Rate
Television						
Radio						
Newspapers						
Magazines						
Yellow Pages						
Printed Promotional Materials						
Direct Mail						
Outdoor Signs						
Indoor Signs						
Trade Shows and Demonstrations						
PR and Publicity						

Step 6 – Transfer Ownership

15 | Initiating the Sale

Once you are aware of how you might use various media to create customer awareness of your product or service, you must use various approaches to initiate the sale, get the customer to order or buy from you, and deliver the goods or services. Especially if you provide a service, you will need to consider effective sales strategies to promote and develop your business. Your intention in Step 5 was to create an advertising message and identify the advertising media that will most attract potential customers. Your intention in Step 6, transfer ownership, is to have your customers buy your product and receive the value they expect from your advertisement and public relations image.

Customers who become aware of your product or service through various advertising media, passing by your store location, receiving your mail order catalog, and through word-of-mouth still need to make the purchase decision in order for you to make any sales. The best advertisements will only get potential customers to your door. How you make the sale and deliver the product or service with any promised extras is part of the total package you are selling. Successfully carrying out this step in the marketing process will greatly affect sales, now and in the future.

The Purchase Decision

The time a customer takes to make the purchase decision offers you many opportunities. The customer is deciding what and how much to buy at what price, forming impressions and developing attitudes about your business. These impressions and attitudes affect what the customer will say about your product or service to others and whether or not the customer will buy from you now, or in the future.

By the time the customer is in your store or has called to inquire about your product or service, he or she has probably heard about what you have for sale. Maybe an ad caught his or her attention. Perhaps you offered a free seminar, an open house, or a free demonstration to explain your product, or you sent direct-mail coupons good for a free cup of coffee to potential customers. Maybe your service was featured in the human interest section of a newspaper.

Remember that the objective is to make sales by having more than satisfied customers. A satisfied customer will have a good attitude toward your product or service. A satisfied-plus customer will tell others, which may lead to additional sales.

Capitalize on Good First Impressions

You want your advertising to make a good first impression on potential customers — perhaps even persuade them to make the decision to buy. However, if the time between when they make their purchase decision and when they can actually order or buy your product is too long, the customer's resolve to buy your product may weaken.

Consider, for example, a cable company that spends $600 on a television ad that asks customers to "call this minute to get your reduced rates," but is unable to handle all the calls. If the customer gets through but is kicked over to a hold system to wait five to seven minutes before talking to a person, the customer may get frustrated and change his or her mind about ordering. The cable company will survive only as long as it has no competition. If a customer cannot order or buy in a timely fashion, the business will lose the sale.

First impressions are important. By the time your prospective customer gets physically close enough to make the decision to buy, call to place an order, or write a check, he or she already has an impression of your business. The client has a preconceived notion about what the product or service is or looks like. The process of ordering or buying the product adds to the customer's first impression, confirming or changing it.

For example, one furniture store was located in a difficult place to find. The store owners included a map in every ad and put up signs at their location thanking customers for going to the trouble to find the store. The signs also assured customers that this distant location allowed the furniture store to offer lower prices due to lower overhead. With these techniques, the store capitalized on its poor location. It risked getting fewer customers by using the ad space for a map rather than copy, but was rewarded when customers were able to find the place.

Real estate agents are aware of the significance of the first sight impression. They stress "curb appeal." They know that to make the best first impression, the homeowner should cut the lawn, prune trees and shrubs, and paint the outside of the house.

Seminar presenters also know the importance of a good first impression. They are professionally attired. They make an effort to learn attendees' names and make them feel welcome. As attendees' comfort levels increase, so do their feelings of trust for the presenters and the services they provide.

In a retail operation, first impressions are equally important. The salespeople are an important part of this impression. People want to be helped to find what they are after. They don't want to wait once they have decided to buy. Like it or not, a customer finds it difficult to separate the attitudes toward the salesperson from the attitudes formed toward the product or service.

Put Yourself in the Customer's Place

Imagine your most satisfied customers telling someone else about purchasing your product or service. What would they say? How would they describe it?

How customers view the total sales process may be critical to achieving a clear market position among competitors. The many ways a product is packaged and displayed — its logo, sales or office environment, window and point-of-purchase displays, location, advertising media, and sales representatives — all affect sales now and in the long run. How would you like a telemarketer, retailer, or service provider to deliver a sales pitch to you? How would their individual sales approaches invite you to make a purchase?

Beware of sales sins that customers will neither forget nor forgive — for example, not knowing the product's price, or deliberately lying about a delivery schedule just to make a quick sale. Some sales sins may be unique to your business. Consider how words and phrases in your advertising copy can be nonoffensive and politically correct to buyers. Think about your sales approach carefully so that you can avoid problems and make a good impression on your customer.

Personal Selling

Personal selling is an especially useful tool that allows you to cater to individual customer's needs and problems. If you or your salesperson has well-developed product knowledge or can easily explain how your product or service will benefit a particular situation, your customer will make the purchase with greater ease and confidence.

Many businesses rely heavily on personal selling as a large part of their marketing strategy, and many small businesses emphasize effective personal selling. For example, they use company sales representatives and point-of-purchase salespeople to identify potential customers and act as consultants in satisfying particular client needs. Personal selling is often what distinguishes some businesses from others, especially larger competitors. The salesperson is in a position to make or break the potential sale, depending on whether the salesperson knows the product, can perceive the customer's needs, and has a manner of selling that is effective both in putting the customer at ease and in closing the sale.

Effective personal selling is shown to influence the purchase decision primarily for convenience goods, impulse items, and services. Personal selling is often a major factor in influencing the purchase of shopping, specialty, and industrial goods and services. It usually plays a role when customers are interested in the product or service but not knowledgeable enough about the offering.

Knowledge Is Power for Salespeople

Salespeople who know a great deal about the product or service, are knowledgeable about people, and can effectively demonstrate the product are a real asset. You can assure that you and your sales staff are well trained by establishing a training program that might include sales meetings, seminars, conventions, and on-the-job sales training. A well-trained staff is not only more effective with individual sales, but also adds to a positive and professional company image.

Knowledgeable sales personnel generate more trust and confidence from their customers. Knowledge will help project a desirable image of your company when it comes time for your customers to do repeat buying. For many types of products and services, such as life insurance, clothing, or computers, sales representatives are the point of contact that clients or customers seek when they are in the market to repurchase. A good salesperson is in the position to make suggestions of product and service benefits that the customer is still unaware of, despite your other advertising and sales promotion efforts. A suggestion from sales personnel who know their customers by name gives the customer a sense of personal attention in a fast-paced world. Salespeople should be trained to listen, observe, assist, and consult the customer during the buying decision. Their insights and product or service knowledge, including any ads, coupons, or special offers you are currently advertising and promoting, can greatly affect sales.

Effective Personal Selling

Effective personal selling has the distinct advantage of allowing you to get immediate feedback from the customer when he or she makes the purchase. You can conduct on-the-spot market research through good customer relations and effective personal selling. You gain a continual flow of valuable information to improve sales training, image development, and the particular words and images you use in other advertising media.

Personal selling has many other advantages as an effective part of your overall marketing process. Consider some of these advantages to using personal selling as part of your marketing campaign.

- Salespeople can explain product or service benefits in a professional, consultative manner that caters to potential customers' individual needs while making them feel important.
- One-on-one communication between buyer and seller can help overcome any doubts, questions, or objections the potential customer may have.
- Personal selling is especially beneficial for promoting services and goods that need special explanation, installation, customization, or trade-ins.
- The salesperson can utilize effective personal selling skills before, during, and after the actual sale. Using personal selling techniques can help reinforce your overall company image, repeat sales, and good word-of-mouth advertising.
- Personal selling can help the customer recognize your product's intangible benefits and see them as a tangible incentive to purchase now rather than later.
- Personal selling helps develop satisfied-plus customers who can effectively increase sales potential through word-of-mouth advertising.

No matter how much advertising and public relations you have done, you may need effective personal selling to support the promised and proclaimed benefits of your product or service. If your sales force is not effective, your other advertising efforts may fail also. Consider that, just as personal selling can influence sales in a positive way, sales personnel who are not informed or who don't know how to present the product or close a sale can negatively affect your sales potential.

If personal selling represents a large part of your marketing effort, sales personnel need to be able to handle customer complaints, as well as sales, to maintain good customer relations. To develop an effective sales approach, fill out Worksheet 22, Effective Personal Selling, at the end of this chapter.

Planning Effective Outside Sales Calls

You can include in your personal selling efforts visits, or calls, to your customers. A great deal of personal selling goes on when you are the person traveling to on-site premises as the service provider or company representative. For example, if you are a management consultant who has been called to a hospital to give a presentation or workshop, knowing as much as possible about your potential client can help you provide a more meaningful experience for hospital staff. Being as knowledgeable as possible ahead of time is one way to build an effective marketing strategy. Always try to do a little research about your potential client before making the sales call.

If you plan to include outside sales calls in your marketing plan, photocopy several blanks of Worksheet 23, Sales Call Planning Guide, at the end of this chapter. You can then fill in one for your first customer, or type of customer group, and take it with you on your outside sales calls.

Selling Services – A Special Case

Several special characteristics of the service sector require service providers to work a little harder to differentiate their service package. All services and most products have both tangible and intangible benefits as perceived by potential customers. You can usually directly experience tangible benefits — you can see, smell, taste, touch, or test them. Intangible benefits, on the other hand, relate more directly to a projected image.

Marketing a service means marketing an intangible. Service is sold according to promises and expectations made. Since intangible benefits are difficult to relate to, word-of-mouth from satisfied customers is a vital tool to teach other customers what intangible benefits your product provides. Word-of-mouth and effective personal sales efforts are essential ingredients for marketing services successfully. If Joe's Tax Service claimed to be able to save you tax dollars, you may not believe Joe, but you would believe someone who had experienced the service before and perceived the claim to be true.

Customers can often postpone purchasing a service or perform the service themselves, such as doing their own bookkeeping, taxes, or gardening. Advertising appeals that communicate to potential customers how your service can alleviate problems now, or bring more convenience into their lives in the immediate present, can help you make the sale.

A service business may attract customers primarily from a local area. You may need to use the Yellow Pages or a descriptive business card, flyer, or brochure to market your service. Provide a means of personal identification with your service — a unique motto, a captive logo. Some type of personal identifier will help attract and keep loyal customers. Of course, provide the quality of service expected, too.

To sell a service, sell it with confidence and tact. Selling a service often requires a more certain, yet subtle approach to your potential customer. If you can make a client feel comfortable purchasing your services and satisfied with the results he or she was led to expect, you have a satisfied customer. In addition, the customer will be a good source of testimonials to help encourage repeat buying and word-of-mouth advertising among friends and associates — the satisfied-plus element you seek from your marketing efforts.

Word-of-mouth advertising is its own form of personal selling. When a customer receives a recommendation from a friend or co-worker about your service, that customer will feel more secure about purchasing the service. Even if you only use referrals and storefront or office signage to attract customers, good word-of-mouth advertising can mean the difference between mediocre sales and a growing clientele.

As you develop your marketing and advertising campaign, with a constant eye to acquiring satisfied-plus customers, remember five things you want to advertise by word-of-mouth:

- Where and when your service is available;
- What specific or special services you provide;
- The quality of performance customers can expect;
- Any guarantees you offer; and
- How the results of using your service will directly benefit potential customers.

If you can communicate these more tangible service features and benefits to your existing customers, and get those customers to spread the word, you will have a good chance of effectively marketing and selling the intangible features and benefits of your service as well.

Initiating the Sale Summary

Successful marketing is more than making potential customers aware of your product or service — it is making the sale. When you carefully consider how you can create a good impression and help customers decide to buy, you will build a successful marketing strategy.

Just as important as the impression you make when you initiate a sale is the impression you make when the customer orders, buys, or receives the product — when the customer takes possession of the product. Chapter 16, Order, Buy, and Deliver, discusses how you can take advantage of this important part of transferring ownership, Step 6 in your marketing process.

Worksheet 22 – Effective Personal Selling

Successful personal selling requires a great deal of preparation, and you need to know all you can about your prospects — your potential customers. Answer the following questions for your business in the space provided.

Describe your personal selling approach and how you currently use it as a marketing tool for your business. _____

_____

_____

_____

Who or what circumstances might influence your customers' buying decision? _____

_____

_____

_____

Do you expect your customers to make the decision to purchase your product as a group — a family or committee — or as individuals? What difference will this make on your personal selling approach?

_____

_____

_____

To improve your sales presentation, what would be useful information to know about your:

Prospective customer? _____

_____

_____

Product or service (such as benefits or features your product offers)? _____

_____

_____

Competition? _____

_____

_____

Industry trends? _____

_____

_____

Worksheet 23 – Sales Call Planning Guide

In the space provided, monitor each of the sales calls you make to customers. You may want to photocopy this worksheet and have blanks to fill in for each sales call you make. Sales call planning assures effective follow up on sales leads.

Date: _____   Company: _____

Address: _____   Type of Business: _____

Key Contact: _____   Phone: _____

Position: _____   Referred by: _____

Key Decision Maker: _____   Position: _____

If the key contact is not the decision maker, how best can the key contact be utilized? _____

_____

The decision-making process is described as follows: _____

_____

_____

The potential needs of the customer are: _____

_____

How can you help this prospect better than other competitors? _____

_____

_____

Your objectives of this sales call or presentation are: _____

_____

_____

Possible responses you may receive from prospects include: _____

_____

Supporting documentation displays, materials, or people needed on call include: _____

_____

_____

Follow up required — actions and times: _____

_____

_____

16 | Order, Buy, and Deliver

When a customer purchases your product or service — actually takes out his or her wallet or fills out an order form — you have yet another critical opportunity to win a satisfied-plus customer. The moment the customer orders or buys the product and takes possession of it is vital to the marketing process. You want your customer to take ownership of the product with a positive feeling that he or she has made the right decision, that the product will perform as expected. Furthermore, you want the customer to translate those positive feelings into word-of-mouth advertising for your business. Transferring ownership, Step 6 in the marketing process, is an opportunity to secure satisfied-plus customers that your business cannot afford to miss.

You can capitalize on the order or buy moment in several ways. This chapter discusses methods for point-of-purchase selling, such as recommending additional products that complement what the customer just bought. You will also learn how to make the delivery of your product or service part of your overall marketing strategy rather than an afterthought. Finally, this chapter describes strategies for turning the order, buy, and deliver steps of the marketing process into the precursors of a successful customer follow-up campaign.

Delivering a Product

If you offer delivery as part of a purchase, you can include some very simple techniques in your delivery process that will increase customer satisfaction.

If you are going to deliver the product, be sure it is set up and functioning properly before the delivery person leaves. For example, if you sell and deliver a piano, play a tune on the piano; make certain the piano is in tune and all the keys and pedals are operating. Leave a free music book as a thank you. If you are delivering a computer, don't leave until the person who has purchased it knows how to do at least a few things on it.

Make certain it is working. Many dissatisfied microcomputer customers dump their current supplier as soon as they discover a competitor they like better, primarily because the supplier provides the necessary training to help them effectively use the product. Many businesses can differentiate themselves from the competition by providing the needed or promised training.

For some high-priced items, you may want to take a picture of the product after you deliver it with an instant developing camera. Have the owner in the picture too. This could be helpful to the buyer for insurance purposes and give him or her good feelings about the new purchase.

Counteract Buyer Regret

Consider that you have just been handed the money or signed the contract to provide a product or service. The customer needs reassurance that this was a wise decision — a moment when the client or customer might think, "Did I make the right decision?" At that instant, you should make some reassuring remarks, such as, "Thank you for your purchase. I'm certain you will get many years of carefree service from XYZ. We've had excellent feedback on it."

Buyer regret can be a serious detriment to your marketing goals. Often, buyer regret is not the fault of the business owner. Customers will sometimes buy more than they can really afford, or buy an impulse item they really don't want. No matter what the reason for buyer regret, your job is to counteract it with words of encouragement, reassurance, and gratitude.

Consider, for example, that you have just chopped three inches off your young customer's hair. Up comes the mirror. "That really shows off your fine features." Give assurance; make a positive statement. The order or buy moment may be your only chance to thank your customer for buying from you and give assurance that the purchase was wise — key ingredients in a successful marketing strategy.

Point-of-Purchase Selling

In addition to reassuring the customer when you deliver the product or service, you may want to do some point-of-purchase selling, especially if you operate a retail business. Point-of-purchase selling can be helpful to the customer. For example, after you sell a piece of clothing for which the customer may not have the right color shoes, you might ask, "Would you like some shoes to match this?" The customer may be very grateful for the suggestion.

However, point-of-purchase selling can also be annoying to the customer. Remember, you want to develop a long-term relationship with the customer. If you suggest something the customer may really need, do it; if you are being pushy, forget it.

Delivering a Service

How you produce or deliver a service must be appropriate to your service profession. A customer who pays $400 per day for a management seminar expects the presenter to be professionally attired. You also want to deliver the service in a timely fashion. A professional service person who keeps customers waiting gives the wrong message — a message that the professional's time is more important than the client's. Some doctors, dentists, attorneys, opticians, and other service professionals make a point never to keep their clients waiting. They may earn a dollar or two less per day by not scheduling so closely, but they are more likely to have satisfied-plus customers, loyal clients who will continue to use the same service professionals regardless of the ups and downs of the economy.

Customers often assess the value or worth of a service while it is being delivered or performed. If the doctor or lawyer moves authoritatively and speaks with conviction, or the psychoanalyst reels off crisp scenarios while performing his or her services, you will likely feel more comfortable, self-assured, and satisfied.

Many service businesses acquire and keep loyal customers by letting their customers set an approximate hour rather than an approximate day or half-day for when they can expect the delivery. These service businesses send the message, "We know your time is important."

When you do something extra for your customer, such as make them a free offer or upgrade their purchase for little or nothing in return, you are making a marketing investment. Customers expect good service; you have to give them more than they expect to create satisfied-plus customers. If you sell a pair of eyeglasses, offer a couple of free cases. When you prepare your client's income taxes, offer a free form on which your client can keep track of income and expenses for the next year to make tax figuring easier.

You want your customer to feel good about receiving your service. It is completely appropriate for you to ask your customer for referrals or for a testimonial you could use in your advertising. Put on your thinking cap to find ways you can create a satisfied customer who would just as soon help you because you have just helped him or her.

⇨   The Evergreen Indoor Plant Nursery needs to develop a strategy for delivering the product — both the plants and the consultation service — that leaves customers reassured and comfortable with their purchase. The market research Paul and Ellen did in Step 2 of their marketing process showed that people who buy plants often worry about the plants becoming diseased or dying. Research indicates that this fear may be so great that people will decide not to buy plants, or buy silk flowers or plastic plants instead. Paul and Ellen think they can counteract this customer fear with some specific and simple techniques.

First, Evergreen will solicit testimonials from customers who have been pleased with their purchases. The testimonials will be available at the nursery for customers who come in to browse. They will also be included as part of Evergreen's brochure and point-of-purchase sales materials. The endorsements from past customers that their plants have survived and thrived over many years should be very reassuring to future Evergreen customers.

Second, Evergreen will offer its customers a plant maintenance contract. As part of the contract, Evergreen will agree that plants that die while under the maintenance contract will be replaced at no cost.

Third, after delivering a large order to an office or commercial building, Evergreen will take a photograph of the office that shows off the plants. The owners will send the photo, along with a thank you note, to the customer.

In addition, Evergreen wants to make sure that large purchasers are able to buy the quantities they desire with little trouble. Evergreen will therefore accommodate credit card purchases and carry invoiced accounts for long-standing clients.

Order, Buy, and Deliver Summary

Just as the Evergreen Indoor Plant Nursery has worked out a targeted strategy for Step 6, transfer of ownership, you need to consider how you can plan successful methods for the order and delivery of your product or service. Worksheet 24, Delivering the Product or Service, at the end of this chapter will help you. A successful and well-planned transfer of ownership for your product or service will lead directly to a successful follow-up campaign, which is Step 7 in your marketing process.

Worksheet 24 – Delivering the Product or Service

When you deliver your product or service, you have an important opportunity to assure customer satisfaction-plus. You or your staff has direct contact with the customer, and that direct contact will leave a lasting impression on the customer. As you read the questions below, consider how this vital step in your marketing process can be used to assure customer satisfaction-plus.

Describe how the delivery or performance of your service affects customers' perception of what the service is worth? How can this help build repeat customers? _____

_____

_____

_____

What can you do at the point-of-purchase display or during the process of delivery to help assure the customer that he or she has made the right choice? _____

_____

_____

_____

_____

What appeals or benefits might you especially emphasize during the sale to help ensure that the customer actually makes the purchase decision? How will you assure that the product or service is delivered on time and as promised? _____

_____

_____

_____

Describe below how word-of-mouth advertising can work for you. If you provide a service, can you ask for a referral? How would you use the referral? _____

_____

_____

_____

What could you do to improve the quality of your product or service and encourage more word-of-mouth advertising? _____

_____

_____

_____

_____

Step 7 – Follow Up and Obtain Feedback

Chapter 17

Reinforce Customer Satisfaction-Plus

17 | Reinforce Customer Satisfaction-Plus

The best advertisements in the world will only bring customers to your door. After that, it is your responsibility to keep your customers satisfied so they will come back again. Without satisfied customers, no business has a future. However, customers expect to be satisfied. To get customers to come back, to be repeat customers, to tell others about your business, and to refrain from trying out your competitors, you must deliver more than satisfaction — you must deliver customer satisfaction-plus.

Every step in your marketing process is geared to getting and keeping satisfied-plus customers. Step 7, to follow up and obtain feedback, is designed to encourage and reinforce customer satisfaction with your product and your business. By the time you are ready to follow up with customers, they should already be satisfied with the price, delivery, and use of the product. Your follow-up campaign will merely reinforce the customer's sense of satisfaction he or she has already experienced. Make sure customers understand how to use the product, that the service provided has lasting value, and that customers feel satisfied by the intangible product benefits they expected. Customer follow up ensures future sales and continued word-of-mouth advertising — it reinforces customer satisfaction-plus.

This final step in your marketing process is critical for securing repeat customers, customer referrals, new customers, and new product ideas. Your follow-up campaign, laid out in this chapter and in the two worksheets that follow, will assure that customers remember your product and your business, and the satisfaction they experienced when they bought from you. The satisfied-plus customer is the key to marketing success.

A Successful Follow-Up Campaign

If you follow the seven step marketing process carefully, your follow-up campaign will lead to satisfied-plus customers, referrals, and new customers. Your follow-up campaign is also your main source for input on how your marketing strategy works. The six primary goals of any successful follow-up campaign are to:

- Follow up with customers to make sure they are pleased with the product and its performance;
- Ask for referrals and testimonials;
- Advertise and promote your business;
- Encourage word-of-mouth advertising;
- Solicit input for new product and service ideas or product modifications; and
- Determine or verify the effectiveness of your overall marketing strategy.

These six critical aspects of a successful follow-up campaign are outlined in greater detail below. Worksheet 25, Customer Satisfaction Update, at the end of this chapter will help you plan your follow-up strategy and gear it toward acquiring satisfied-plus customers.

Follow-Up Contact with Customers

The first step in a successful follow-up campaign is to make sure customers are able to use your product effectively and successfully. Your customers often like hearing again how important they are to you and that you are concerned about providing a quality product or service for their use and enjoyment. A follow-up phone call encourages them to tell the truth about their experience with the product shortly after they have tried it out. Is the product's quality what your customers want and expect? What else can you do to ensure the product's quality use or your customers' enjoyment of it? Is their experience with your product or service positive? Point-of-purchase demonstrations and great personal selling are not enough.

Many products, and some services, are used inadequately, infrequently, or sometimes not at all. Customers tend to feel angry and guilty for not getting the use out of a product they recently bought. Those feelings often translate into negative feelings toward the manufacturer, retail outlet, or service provider. If your customers develop negative feelings toward your product, service, or business in general, you will lose the positive word-of-mouth advertising you want, and you may even experience some negative publicity. Using a follow-up phone call or brief in-person survey questionnaire can help overcome these negative experiences.

Consider, for example, a computer sales outfit that telephones its customers a few days or even a month after delivery. This store is on the right track. The time to follow up is after the product has been delivered and the customer has had time to use it. Is the customer able to get the programs to work? Let the customer know of any changes or updates that might have occurred recently or any available training seminars. This follow up builds long-term success.

Follow-Up Referrals

You can also use this follow-up contact time to ask for referrals and product endorsements. Satisfied-plus customers are your best and least expensive form of advertising to help your business grow. Many customers who feel satisfied-plus love to tell their friends, family, and business associates about products and services they feel good about. Ask if others in the customer's household or place of business are also interested in learning how to use the product?

Sometimes, customers may be so enthusiastic about your product or service that they would feel comfortable appearing in a future advertising appeal you may make, such as television spots or newspaper product endorsements. All this follow up helps tremendously to support your business' image of high quality and genuine customer concern. Satisfied-plus customers are eager to see you succeed in business so they can continue to support you.

Follow Up as Advertising and Customer Relations

A phone call to find out how your customer's experience is with the product is, in effect, additional advertising. A follow-up phone call reassures the customer that he or she made a good purchase. Use the follow-up stage to send copies of your latest advertising or additional information on related ideas, products, or services to your customers.

Another way you can follow up with your customers is to mail a thank-you note a week or two after purchase. Enclose with the thank-you note a customer evaluation questionnaire and a stamped self-addressed envelope. Ask in the questionnaire how the customer liked the product or service. What could be improved? If it is appropriate to offer a discount coupon for such a valued customer, enclose one.

More and more, businesses are using a 24-hour-a-day hot-line phone service. If you can't have a person available all the time to answer the phone, get an answering service or voice mail. Ask customers to express their concerns and treat those concerns with respect. A television cable outfit that gets a call for service on Friday afternoon, but responds with, "I'm sorry, we cannot get a repair person to you until Monday," is begging the customer to turn to a competitor.

You may want to let customers know of other related items or sales they might be interested in. Is there an article on the future of computers that might be of interest? Send out copies. Is there a better floppy disk than what came with the original sale? Send a coupon good for one free blank disk or toward a $5 discount on a package of ten.

Encourage Word-of-Mouth Advertising

The actual cost of securing a new customer is often high. Your best sources for developing new customers and increased sales come from current satisfied customers, and from enthusiastic employees. You can do numerous things to help ensure that customers will buy again and that customers and employees tell others favorable things about your product or service. Consider some of the following ideas and how they might apply to your product.

- After a sales call, use a stamped, self-addressed return card listing three different times and days from which the customer may choose to make an appointment.

- Send a reminder card to customers regarding warranties or yearly appointments.

- Send a customer survey to customers on your mailing list or those you have researched in person, on-site, to see how they are doing and which additional products or services they might be interested in. Refer to the Sample Customer Profile Survey in Chapter 6, page 63.

- Use a direct-mail campaign to distribute coupons good at local merchants and dealers; for example, an appliance store might send out coupons for a free pint of berries from a local market to all customers who purchased an ice-cream maker last year.

- Give out free samples of your product; for example, a garden center might send a blooming two-inch marigold to last year's customers, or a bakery might have miniature cookies next to its cash register.

- Help support the local theater or symphony by purchasing groups of tickets at a discount and then passing that discount on to interested customers.

- Offer classes on your premises that may be of special interest to customers, such as a homebuilder class at the local lumber outlet or a CPR class to a local shopping center's clientele.

- Announce to your clientele an upcoming television special that deals with the particular service you provide.

- Have a special pre-sale for preferred customers before announcing it on local radio stations and newspapers, such as a furniture store-moving sale.

You can also offer your customers guarantees as a method of customer follow up. Whether you have actually offered a product or service guarantee, dollar amount, or time limit — such as "your money refunded if not completely satisfied," "double your money back if you don't get complete satisfaction, no questions asked," or "a fully-refundable 30-day money back guarantee" — some kind of guarantee is usually implied. However, you can state your guarantee policy more explicitly, and use your follow-up calls as ways to remind customers that you stand behind your product.

Of course, you need to make sure your guarantees are feasible and profitable for you. If you have a business policy stating that you won't be undersold, and someone comes to your store with an ad showing a recently purchased product for sale less elsewhere, you need to honor your ad to get continued business from that person — and their friends. If that policy turns out not to be profitable for you, you will need to change it and differentiate your product on other nonprice factors.

Ask for New Product Ideas

During follow up is the perfect time to ask customers for new product ideas. Often, a customer knows what he or she wants, but cannot find it on the market, or cannot find it in your store and must turn to one of your competitors.

If you ask customers for the products or services they are looking for, you may be able to stay on the cutting edge of new product trends, or to capitalize on a new fashion that your competitors are not yet aware of. Asking your customers for new product ideas and what they want from you can help expand your market niche.

Verify the Effectiveness of Your Marketing Campaign

If you use follow-up techniques successfully, you will obtain valuable customer feedback about your product or service, your business, your advertising methods, your pricing, location, distribution, packaging, and your sales and delivery — about all the previous steps in your marketing process.

Following up and obtaining customer feedback is the major way to ensure that your marketing process is responsive to changes in the marketplace and in your customer base. This vital seventh step brings your process back to the beginning, allowing you to reevaluate the marketing decisions you have made and to keep up with a changing business environment. Look at how the Evergreen Indoor Plant Nursery has prepared for its follow-up campaign.

⇨ Evergreen Indoor Plant Nursery is well positioned to develop a successful follow-up campaign. Paul and Ellen have already decided, as part of their delivery process, that they will take pictures of their customers' offices after placing all the new plants. To invite feedback from their customers, they will send a questionnaire, along with the photograph, to customers shortly after the sale is complete. The questionnaire will focus on four concerns:

- How the customer likes the new plants and feels about the office with the new plants in it;

- Whether the customer knows anyone who would be interested in the service and products Evergreen offers;
- Whether the customer has any suggestions for new products or services Evergreen could provide to current or future customers;
- Any changes Evergreen should make in its marketing plan, such as price, advertising, or product image; and
- The level of satisfaction the customer has in the purchasing process he or she has just been through, along with any suggestions.

For some of Evergreen's larger customers, Paul and Ellen would like to give a free, unique watering container or a new, small plant, along with the follow-up questionnaire, or a follow-up phone call or visit.

As the Evergreen Indoor Plant Nursery illustrates, a well-planned marketing process leading up to Step 7 will make successful follow up all the easier. When you establish good rapport with your customers, and satisfy them at every step of your marketing process, they will gladly provide you with feedback, including customer referrals and new product ideas.

The Consumer Diary Approach

Often, the best way to have effective follow up is to look at your business from the customer's point of view. You can do this by using the consumer diary approach. Put yourself in the customer's place. For one week, propose to employees, if you have them, that everyone keep consumer diaries they can discuss after work, at a staff meeting, over a cup of coffee, or at a training session. If you operate alone or out of your home, just do this exercise by yourself and use it to check out how your competitors and non-competitors do effective business and how they keep satisfied customers.

The object of this exercise is to get you and your employees into a consumer-oriented frame of mind. Record two or three consumer experiences you have during the week. They might include shopping for groceries, getting gas, getting a hair cut, or ordering from a catalog. Then act as a consultant to the owner of the business involved. How would you recommend the consumer's experience be improved? What did the business do well? This is an on-paper activity. When everyone gets together, each can read his or her worst and best examples.

Get into the habit of looking for practices which make a positive and negative impression on the customer. What was happening when you felt more than satisfied with a consumer experience or with a product or service? As you discuss this exercise, it may become all too clear that the majority of the experiences recorded are negative. Apply what you learn to making sure your customers' experiences are positive. Worksheet 26, How to Maximize Customer Satisfaction, at the end of this chapter will help you focus on what actions you can take to make sure your customers are satisfied-plus.

Customer Satisfaction-Plus Summary

On page 206 is a sample of the Evergreen Indoor Plant Nursery's seven step marketing process outline. Worksheet 27, Your Marketing Process Outline, on the following page, is a blank outline for you to fill in your own marketing strategies. Make some photocopies of this worksheet for use when you rework your marketing process in the future.

Now that you have planned and prepared for your marketing process, you are ready to put your process into action. The concluding section of this book, Design Your Marketing Campaign, guides you through goal setting, budgeting, and preparing for the potential national and international growth of your business. With the techniques you have learned so far, and your seven step marketing outline filled in, your marketing goals should come quickly into view.

Worksheet 25 – Customer Satisfaction Update

Is your product or service being experienced favorably or unfavorably? How will you find out? _____

_____

_____

_____

_____

Describe a way that will systematically help you follow up on a customer within two weeks of delivery of purchase. How do you plan to follow up on referrals and leads? _____

_____

_____

_____

_____

Describe any recent updates in your product or service offering that previous customers should know about.

_____

_____

_____

_____

_____

What items can you suggest to complement the product or service a customer recently purchased? What else might become a part of developing a favorable image? _____

_____

_____

_____

_____

Have you checked to see that your salespeople are knowledgeable and enthusiastic about your product or service? _____

_____

_____

_____

_____

Worksheet 26 – How to Maximize Customer Satisfaction

1. Describe your response to the customer when he or she places an order. _____

   _____

   _____

   _____

2. Is your location easy to find? Would a map help? _____

   _____

   _____

   _____

3. List any ideas that are appropriate for your product or service to help secure satisfied-plus customers. _____

   _____

   _____

4. What extra service can you offer customers? _____

   _____

   _____

5. Is there a way you can upgrade a customer's purchase at little or no extra cost? How can you offer your customers a so-called baker's dozen, 13 for the price of 12? _____

   _____

   _____

   _____

6. What first impression does your product or service give? _____

   _____

   _____

   _____

7. What can you do to reassure customers at the point of purchase? How can you maximize your customers' satisfaction with your product or service to make sure they are satisfied-plus?

   _____

   _____

   _____

Sample Marketing Process Outline – Evergreen Indoor Plant Nursery

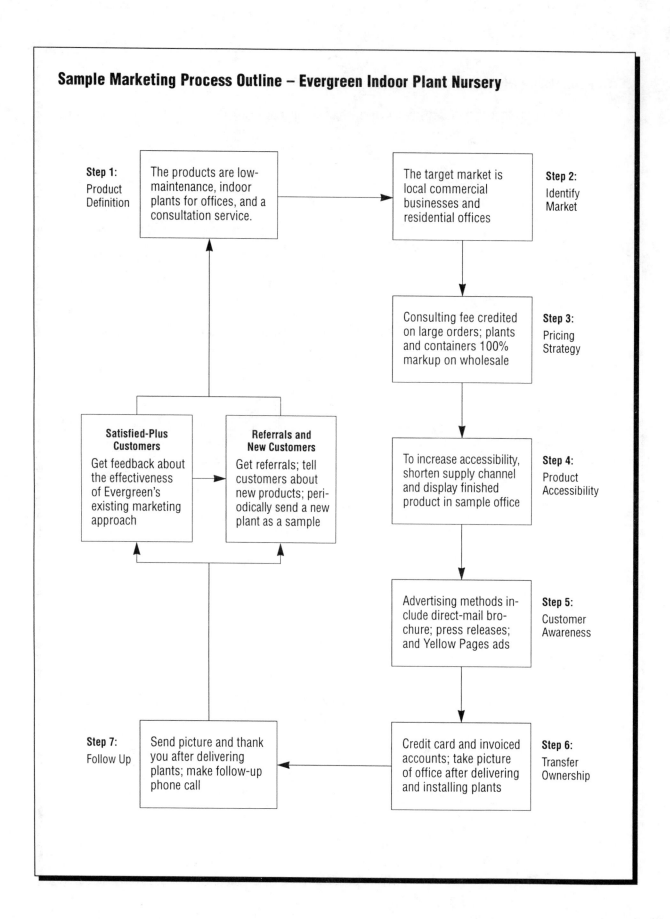

Step 1:
Product
Definition

The products are low-maintenance, indoor plants for offices, and a consultation service.

The target market is local commercial businesses and residential offices

Step 2:
Identify
Market

Consulting fee credited on large orders; plants and containers 100% markup on wholesale

Step 3:
Pricing
Strategy

Satisfied-Plus Customers

Get feedback about the effectiveness of Evergreen's existing marketing approach

Referrals and New Customers

Get referrals; tell customers about new products; periodically send a new plant as a sample

To increase accessibility, shorten supply channel and display finished product in sample office

Step 4:
Product
Accessibility

Advertising methods include direct-mail brochure; press releases; and Yellow Pages ads

Step 5:
Customer
Awareness

Step 7:
Follow Up

Send picture and thank you after delivering plants; make follow-up phone call

Credit card and invoiced accounts; take picture of office after delivering and installing plants

Step 6:
Transfer
Ownership

Worksheet 27 – Your Marketing Process Outline

In the space below, outline your own marketing process as you envision it now. You may want to make copies of this worksheet for use when you reevaluate your marketing process in the future.

Step 1:
Product
Definition

Step 2:
Identify
Market

Step 3:
Pricing
Strategy

Step 4:
Product
Accessibility

Step 5:
Customer
Awareness

Step 6:
Transfer
Ownership

Step 7:
Follow Up

Satisfied-Plus
Customers

Referrals and
New Customers

Conclusion – Design Your Marketing Campaign

18 | Set Goals

Now that you have worked through the basic seven step marketing process, you are ready to put that process into action by designing an effective marketing campaign. A key ingredient to a successful marketing process is setting realistic and attainable goals. When you introduce a new product or service into the marketplace, begin by setting your goals; then plan to achieve those goals by developing a good marketing plan and acquiring satisfied customers.

Depending on what your personal, business, and sales objectives are, the right marketing strategy can help you achieve your goals affordably. A successful marketing campaign is an ongoing process that constantly evaluates and reevaluates all seven steps covered in this book. This seven step marketing process will continually expose your products and services to the marketplace if you design it properly.

Writing a Goals Statement

Marketing goals answer the question, "What results do you expect to achieve from the marketing strategy you will develop during the next year in such areas as sales, market share, growth, profit, and possible diversification?" Take the time now to address that question. Worksheet 28, Setting Your Sales and Marketing Goals, at the end of this chapter provides space to write your goals statement.

In your goals statement, you want to address several issues about your business, your product, and your position in the marketplace, including:

- Sales — Your expected sales for the coming year in gross dollar amount;
- Market share — The percentage of total sales for similar products or services that your business can claim;
- Growth — The expected percentage increase in your annual sales;
- Profitability — The increase or decrease in direct or indirect costs; and
- Diversification potential — The increase in products or services offered.

You also want to consider how you will attain your goals. Reconsider the special features or benefits you identified in your product. Return to Step 1, where you identified what is particularly marketable about your product, defined your product, and wrote a product profile. Look again at worksheets 2, 3, and 4 at the end of Chapter 3 to review your product profile.

Finally, as you consider your sales and marketing goals, try to go beyond the next year or two to consider your long-term goals. How do you plan to remain competitive over the next 10 to 20 years? What changes in business operations will you have to consider? If you work out of your home now, do you anticipate moving to an office at some point in the future? If you can only afford newspaper advertising now, will you eventually purchase television advertising time? Sometimes, long-term marketing goals may simply be to maintain or improve customer relations.

The goals you set will be tremendously important to writing a marketing budget, the subject of Chapter 19. Consider how you will budget your funds now to attain your sales and marketing goals. If you think less expensive advertising now will help establish you in the local marketplace, can you save money for national or international advertising later? You will need to make some long-term sales forecasts to adequately prepare for the future.

Sales Forecasting

Your annual advertising and promotional budget is closely linked to sales goals for the upcoming year. Sales goals, in turn, are influenced by personal and overall organizational goals, the availability of competing products and services, the relative newness of your product or service, and many other factors.

The purpose of any media plan is to develop an effective media strategy and sufficient budget to accomplish the coming year's sales goals. Understanding and clarifying your current marketing objectives and proposed media strategy can help you develop a marketing plan that can serve as a yardstick for assessing future marketing strategy.

Sales forecasts influence budget expenditures, as do goals, competition, and media selection. Before finalizing this coming year's budget, evaluate the various strategies and combinations of media and sales promotion techniques in your marketing campaign. Set performance standards in each area of promotion to determine the effectiveness of dollars spent in each area. Also, monitor feedback in relation to sales and image created through advertising and promotional efforts. All these factors contribute to having an effective media plan that is organized, yet flexible enough to help you accomplish your marketing objectives.

Measuring Customer Response to Your Advertising

As you assess the feasibility of your marketing goals, you will need to examine how your customers respond to your current marketing efforts. One of the most important variables in assembling marketing goals and budgets is to learn the best method for reaching customers. You need to know how much money you spent on advertising per customer reached, measured in cost per thousand (CPM). If you find that with your current marketing efforts you are not able to attain your goals, you will have to change your marketing process, or change your goals.

Several techniques are useful for measuring customer response to media used, message content, sales promotions, sales presentations, and publicity. Using coupons in newspaper and magazine ads and in direct-mail campaigns is an excellent method for comparing your audience reached, the CPM to sales response. Keeping a file on your ads and your competitors' ads helps keep track of which ads best attract customers, and which pictures, benefits, copy message, and layout works best.

Using an on-the-spot market research survey to ask customers and passers-by what they think, prefer, buy, like the most, or need can develop sales potential. Update your customer profile and find new target markets to explore. Continual market research is an invaluable tool in helping you reach target customers and make the best use of your advertising appeals.

As a final note, sometimes concentration on one major advertising medium will affect sales better than just one spot ad in each of several media types. You may want to repeat the same ad layout rather than continually create new ads. For service businesses especially, ask who referred a potential client and follow up on how many sales result from word-of-mouth advertising. Provide a free gift, sample, or hidden message in your advertising as an incentive to respond — a good way to observe the same ad in different media.

⇨ Evergreen Indoor Plant Nursery set some ambitious goals for creating customer awareness of its products and services. Paul and Ellen wanted to attain 25% market share in the local community within two years. According to market research, other nurseries, flower shops, and landscapers did approximately $300,000 in sales last year. Paul and Ellen project that Evergreen can capture $45,000 of that business in the first year, and $75,000 in two years.

Other market research indicates that Evergreen's target market will respond most favorably to good word-of-mouth advertising, competitive pricing, and superior customer service. Evergreen's marketing goals for the first year, therefore, focus on word-of-mouth advertising, a strong emphasis on customer service, coupons and special promotions to bring customers into the nursery, and a public relations campaign that will generate goodwill for the nursery and let the public know about the business.

For the second year, Paul and Ellen plan to expand their advertising to include newspaper ads and radio spots. They anticipate having to increase their marketing budget for the second year, but feel that a campaign of public relations and superior customer service the first year will lay a foundation of customer awareness to complement the radio and newspaper ads the second year.

With first-year sales projections of $45,000, Paul and Ellen are budgeting 5% of sales on marketing, or $2,250, to be spent on training and seminars, price cuts and coupons, and public relations events.

With second-year sales projections of $75,000, Paul and Ellen are budgeting 7% of sales on marketing, or $5,250, to be spent on newspaper and radio ads.

In Chapter 19, you will follow a similar process as Evergreen Indoor Plant Nursery, basing your marketing budget on sales forecasts and the marketing needs dictated by your target market research and sales and marketing goals.

Setting Goals Summary

Advertising and promotional expenses are actually an investment in your business future. The amount of advertising dollars you need to communicate awareness that will result in sales depends on many factors, including:

- What competitors are spending and on which media alternatives;
- Which products or services you should emphasize next year — should you sell out discontinued product lines or promote new fall fashions;
- Changes in the economic, social, political, demographic, and psychological profile of your target customers;
- The location of your business outlet or office — the farther away you are from your target customers, the more it may cost to advertise your location;
- The degree of continuity or ad frequency needed to keep your total image packaging effective — for many products, the customer must see the message several times before they will make a purchase;

- The goals associated with your advertising campaign — whether to increase sales by a certain percent, introduce a new product or service, or maintain good customer relations;
- Whether you need to hire an advertising agency or media consultant; and
- Your intuitive feeling given the influences mentioned above.

Chapter 19 considers these many budgeting variables in detail and provides explanation and worksheets to help you set a marketing budget, track sales, and calculate media effectiveness.

However, the last of these variables, your intuition, may be the most important of all. When introducing a new product or service to the marketplace, use your intuition, along with industry guidelines if they are available, to set goals and determine the right amount to budget and the most advantageous media selection strategy. Estimate the amount you feel necessary or affordable, and then allocate those advertising dollars so that the greatest amount is spent in the first two to six months of creating awareness of the new product or service. Sometimes, all the market research, hired consultants, strategies, and techniques cannot compete with your own gut feeling.

Worksheet 28 – Setting Your Sales and Marketing Goals

Answer the following questions about your business' future growth and sales. The sales and marketing goals you set here will influence your marketing budget for the coming years. On the second page of this worksheet, be sure to consider your long-term goals and how you can tailor your marketing process to achieve them.

What results do you expect during the next year in:

Sales (gross dollar amount)? _____

_____

_____

Market share (percentage of total sales for similar products or services to your buyer segments)? ____

_____

_____

Growth (percentage increase in your annual sales)? _____

_____

_____

Profitability (increase or decrease in direct or indirect costs)? _____

_____

_____

Diversification potential (increase in products/services offered)? _____

_____

_____

Fill in the blanks for your company.

Your target customer groups' characteristics can be described as: _____

_____

_____

The major benefits and features of your product include (see Chapter 3, worksheets 2, 3, and 4): ____

_____

_____

You plan to promote these benefits and features — your marketing advantages — in the following ways:

_____

_____

Worksheet 28 – **Setting Your Sales and Marketing Goals** (continued)

In the future, you can modify or expand your product or service offering, your location, your pricing strategy, and the combination of media, sales promotion ideas, and personal selling strategies to accomplish your long-term goals of _____

_____

_____

_____

_____

_____

_____

_____

_____

_____

_____

_____

_____

_____

_____

_____

_____

_____

_____

_____

_____

_____

_____

_____

_____

_____

_____

_____

_____

_____

_____

19 | Design Your Marketing Budget

Once you have set sales and marketing goals and mapped out your overall marketing plan, including the advertising media you will use, you are ready to prepare a marketing budget.

For many small and large businesses alike, the amount competitors spend on yearly advertising and sales promotion influences their budget decisions and media selections. If you are in a highly competitive market or are promoting commonly purchased goods and services, you need a good strategy for distinguishing your product or service. If you cannot at least meet or exceed your competition's media strategy and dollar expenditure, then you may need to select media that are unlike those of your competitors or use similar media more creatively to help distinguish your product or service. If a corner grocery store cannot compete with the television advertising of a national grocery chain, it could still maintain its presence in the marketplace using well-designed window displays or point-of-purchase free samples.

This chapter analyzes all these different budgeting considerations to ensure that you will:

- Adequately fund your marketing campaign;
- Monitor month-by-month how actual sales match projected sales; and
- Determine the media strategy necessary to create customer awareness of your business and products.

At the end of this chapter, fill in Worksheet 29, Your Advertising Budget Worksheet, to help you with your budget reviews and Worksheet 30, Yearly Sales Forecast and Marketing Budget, to help you monitor sales and marketing budgets from year to year.

Easy Budget Calculations

If you are just starting out, you may want to develop a simple budget estimate based either on annual sales forecasts, or simply on the funds you have left over after meeting all other expenses. You can also develop more sophisticated marketing budgets, including budgets based on the advertising dollars needed to sell one unit. Both methods are described below.

Percentage of Sales

The most easily adaptable and most commonly used method of determining your total advertising and sales promotion budget for the coming year is to apply a certain percentage of sales either to last year's sales, if you were in business, or to expected sales for the coming year. This method is easy to calculate and realistic in approach. For example, if sales last year were $200,000, and you wanted to spend 10% on this year's advertising, you would budget $20,000.

You can adjust the percentage according to whether your objective is, for example, to increase market share or to change the emphasis from advertising to personal selling. Some businesses adjust their budgets according to the seasonal fluctuations of their markets. For example, See's Candy raises its advertising expenditure right before Christmas and Valentine's Day. Retailers who target the back-to-school market advertise heavily right before a new school year begins. Businesses just starting out or launching a new product are wise to increase advertising and promotion dollars during the pre-opening and opening months to help the business get going. Budgeting based on percentage of sales makes budget decisions easy, flexible, and reasonable to calculate.

Residual Funds

Another method to determine your marketing budget is to use the residual funds available after accounting for all other projected expenses. This budgeting method is particularly beneficial if you are starting a new business, because you may need to keep marketing expenses low until sales increase. However, this method can also be very dangerous because you can defeat your sales potential by not spending enough advertising dollars to effectively reach target customers.

You may also want to incorporate into your budgeting strategy research into what your industry as a whole is spending on advertising. Several government agencies and financial institutions publish industry guideline percentages. Check the Internal Revenue Service, the Census report, Dun & Bradstreet, Robert Morris Associates reports, and the Accounting Corporation of America. Most of these are available through your public library or through libraries of media specialists from whom you purchase time and space, or media consultants and advertising agencies that help design your marketing campaign.

Budgeting for Convenience, Shopping, or Specialty Goods

You may want to base your budget calculation on the type of product you sell. For example, convenience goods are purchased frequently and immediately, whereas shopping goods and specialty or unique goods often take more time and effort before the customer decides to purchase. Depending on the type of product you sell, you can vary your budgeting method from using a percentage of sales to using a fixed percentage per unit sold and apply it to projected sales. For example, for large, expensive shopping and specialty goods, such as furs, cars, or jewelry, and services, such as computer programming or interior decorating, you can determine how many advertising dollars are necessary to create one sale, and then develop a percentage you can apply to overall expected sales for the upcoming year.

Stretch Your Marketing Dollars

You can maximize the effectiveness of your advertising budget in many ways. For example, you can convert a specific ad in a newspaper or magazine to a direct mail or publicity piece by having it reproduced and mailed to customer lists or media publicists. Whatever you have already paid for ad layout, photos, design, and art renderings can be reused for a different target audience with little or no additional cost. Cooperative advertising, and the use of advertising professionals can also stretch your marketing dollars, if used correctly.

Cooperative Advertising

Take advantage of any cooperative advertising dollars available for your products. If you have a retail outlet through which products manufactured by others are sold, or a service organization that carries related products, such as a cleaning establishment that has rug shampoo products, it is possible to stretch advertising dollars by cooperating with product manufacturers in running specific ads that are mutually advantageous. The retail outlet or service organization can get advertising expenses reimbursed, often up to 50%, by specifying the manufacturer's logo, product, or product line in their advertising.

Manufacturers often work with retailers in a cooperative advertising effort to boost sales — a win-win approach that stretches your advertising dollars. This form of advertising is often overlooked by small businesses because extra paperwork is always involved — retailers must meet manufacturers' requirements to get reimbursed. Usually, you are required to keep detailed records and send in copies of advertisements — tearsheets —

to get reimbursed. Although this may seem like a hassle for a small business owner with little spare time for paperwork, co-op dollars from supplier sources can boost your promotional effort by as much as 30%! Almost every manufacturer and supplier offers some type of cooperative advertising and free promotional brochures.

Even the smallest retail outlets and service organizations that use manufactured products can benefit. Retailers usually get a better price than manufacturers when buying advertising space and time, so it becomes profitable for the manufacturer to invest cooperative advertising dollars for their products that you sell. Manufacturers will also offer cooperative advertising to retailers as an incentive to start carrying their products. If the product does well, both manufacturer and retailer benefit.

Although arrangements vary, most reimbursements are based on either a percentage of volume the dealer does with the manufacturer or a per-unit allowance on sales made during a specified time period. Since manufacturers who offer cooperative advertising arrangements include the cost in determining the price, at least check into the possibilities — otherwise your potential reimbursement becomes more profit for the manufacturer. Of course, you may find that cooperative advertising is not cost-effective given the manufacturer's requirements.

If you manufacture a product and seek distributors, dealers, and retail outlets, consider cooperative advertising arrangements as incentives. Cooperative advertising is essentially a form of sales promotion. It helps stretch advertising dollars by creating outlets and awareness of your product, which of course can improve your profit.

Although you may want to compare industry standards and collect examples that you see of cooperative advertising arrangements, your best approach may be to develop different requirements. Cooperative advertising requirements may include the use of a logo together with the product name, other limits on the dealer when showing competitive products, or proof that the dealer has actually run the ad in order to qualify for expense reimbursement. Cooperative advertising allows a great deal of flexibility in the arrangements you can structure, although the Federal Trade Commission does prescribe some requirements.

Advertising Agencies and Media Consultants

Advertising and promotional efforts can often be more effective when they are implemented by professionals, such as advertising agents and media consultants. Take advantage of local media representatives, especially newspapers, magazines, and television, to get free advice and assistance in preparing ad copy, design, layout, and correct media timing. Trade associations, the Better Business Bureau, chambers of commerce, and networking organizations are valuable sources of information and assistance when determining an appropriate advertising budget. If you plan to develop and grow your business, add specialists in graphic design, artwork, and ad layout to your list of experts. Printers and direct-mail list brokers can also be helpful with suggestions to stretch advertising efforts.

If you have a $5,000 annual advertising budget, should you hire an advertising agency? Probably not. Most agencies operate on a commission of 15% of what is paid to the media. Charges for out-of-pocket expenses, such as artwork or photography, are also passed on to the client. The agency has to cover direct and indirect costs and make a profit. If the average monthly advertising budget runs about $400 ($5,000 ÷ 12 = $417), the agency's commission is $62.50 a month. You may be able to find a new, small, hungry agency that would be interested, or one with a set fee or fee and commission combination, that you could approach. If you can budget $10,000 to $15,000 per month in advertising, many agencies will be interested. Finding an ad agency is like getting a loan from a bank — the larger the loan the greater the likelihood of getting it.

On the other hand, even with a small budget, you may be wise to use an agency. Burton Baskin and Irvine Robbins approached a small new ad agency with all of $500. It was just after World War II. Baskin and Robbins had started an ice cream business, and two or three small stores were selling their ice cream to retail customers. A large dairy firm tried to stop the store from carrying Baskin and Robbins ice cream. The fledgling Carson-Roberts agency helped them out in the interest of possibly getting a long-term client relationship. They recommended spending the $500 on a fun image — painting pink and chocolate colored balloons on a white background on the delivery trucks and stationery and emphasizing lots of flavors from which to choose. Not bad advice — and the agency grew with its client!

Advertising agencies can help you by selecting the appropriate media and by creating ideas for promoting the business, product, or service. They can also provide technical expertise by writing copy and designing art work. Some agencies will help with marketing research and promotion. The usual advice is to shop around. You can usually negotiate fees or commissions.

Media consultants can offer services at an affordable rate and often be as effective as an advertising agency in helping you create desired results. Advertising agencies and independent media consultants are in business to provide a service — to create awareness of your product or service. You can hire a full-service agency with the talent available to create a total image package — the logo, package design, motto, benefits, photos, film, sound effects, commercial production, layout ad message, image design, and publicity or public relations agent. Media consultants can create press releases and help develop other effective forms of sales promotion materials and creative ideas. On the other hand, you can probably find some of that talent within your circle of associates, family, and friends. You may need only to hire specialists who consult on one major aspect of your marketing campaign, such as a photo layout expert, publicity agent, graphic artist, designer, or printer.

If you want to hire people outside of your organization to assist in marketing your products or services, weigh the cost of their combined talent against the expected results. Agencies derive their income from charging the client or account a flat fee or hourly rate for services or expenses plus a fixed percent. However, they get the majority of their income from media commissions, usually 15% on the cost of time and space purchased through their agency.

For specialized help, or if you have a relatively small advertising budget available, media consultants and smaller agencies are more likely to want your account. Large agencies prefer large accounts that have budgets to match, whereas one person or a small agency is much more willing to cater to individual needs on a smaller budget. Fees are negotiable, so be sure to ask questions and compare several agencies.

In any case, work with someone who has a good feel for your product or service and can create the results you want at a reasonable cost. Likewise, your account must become profitable for the agency or consultant to provide the service you desire and expect. Good communication and feedback are essential for effective use of outside media. Finding the right agent, and following up with the agent to ensure that ads are placed and reaching the most appropriate target customers, can help you have a successful relationship with your media consultant. The overall responsibility remains with you to communicate to the agent the image you want.

Yearly Sales Forecasts and Marketing Budgets

Using good marketing research, your task now is to develop a monthly sales forecast for the next year and annual forecasts for the next three to five years. Of course, market trends and changing economic and other market environment conditions will influence future sales projections. If you are marketing a new product, your major advertising thrust should be in the early stages of product introduction.

A written marketing budget plan will provide a detailed blueprint for how you can achieve sales goals with the promotional efforts you have selected. Worksheet 30, Yearly Sales Forecast and Marketing Budget, at the end of this chapter will give you a yearly blueprint you can monitor for effectiveness as you record your actual monthly sales and compare them to your forecasted sales goals and expectations. Having such a plan for each product or service, or grouping of similar products and services, will help you organize your marketing efforts to achieve maximum results. You may want to photocopy several blanks for different product groups.

Many new businesses count on spending 100% of their normal annual estimated budget during the first four to six weeks of product introduction as an extra effort to create awareness of their new product among competing products. They spend an additional 100% over the next eleven months. These companies budget 200% of their estimated annual advertising budget for the first year so that they can seize a portion of the market for their new product.

A marketing budget plan should take into account the seasonality of the business — its particular sales flow, peaks, and valleys. Be certain that you time advertising and sales promotion efforts so that they coordinate with inventory control and sales personnel. You want your advertising, inventory, and staff to work together to take advantage of seasonal ebbs and flows. For example, hiring extra help around Christmas and for special sales can help create enthusiasm for the product's image and generate greater profitability.

By structuring your media plan and advertising spending to take advantage of proper timing in the marketplace, you will gain invaluable market exposure. Once people become familiar with what you have to offer, the actual quality of the products or services will determine sales, along with continual market research to develop satisfied-plus customers and referrals.

Remember to remain flexible with your media strategy and budget allocations, allowing yourself to make adjustments because of changing market conditions and current business trends, as discussed in Chapter 2. Through careful monitoring of your media plan, you will ensure marketing success, especially when you launch a new product. Monitoring should include comparing projected to actual monthly sales and evaluating the relative effectiveness of various selected media alternatives. When you create your marketing budget, consider the following profit planners:

- Stores that are new, expanding, or in less favorable locations need to budget more for advertising to attract potential customers.

- Service providers should emphasize availability and image to attract clients.

- Strong competition in the marketplace requires you to budget more to attract customers from competitors.

- Stores and service outlets that emphasize lower prices as a major benefit tend to spend more on promotion and advertising than businesses emphasizing other benefits.

- Special dates and events that offer additional sales opportunities need advance budget planning, for example, payroll days of important local businesses, heavy store traffic days, local night openings, tie-ins with national and local merchandising events, new or expanding departments, and inventory reductions at year's end.

Don't hesitate to continue doing market research — ask questions, gather information about potential target customers and the media that best serve them, and gather samples of competitors' advertising and sales promotion ideas for comparison purposes. Recognize investment opportunities in the areas of effective marketing, sales promotion, and media strategy.

Evaluate Your Marketing Plan and Yearly Budget

Overall marketing strategy and sales forecasts need to reflect good, continual research. You need your budget and media strategy to be realistic in light of this research. You need to continually make observations about what is happening in the market. If you clearly state your marketing objectives, you will be able to see if your media and sales promotion strategies are accomplishing your goals. Some media effects are harder to measure than others. Some, like public relations and publicity, are intended more for goodwill and a positive image than directly related to sales. When you evaluate your current marketing plan, consider both your long-term and short-term marketing strategies for promoting your products and services.

Review your budget periodically, every three to six months at least, as you continue to update market information. Be aware of industry guidelines both for typical ad budget as percent of sales and usual media selected. For example, mail-order firms' ad budgets may vary from 18 to 30% of sales while using direct mail, magazines, and television. Auto supply shops may have a typical ad budget closer to 1 to 2% and use direct mail, flyers, newspapers, and the Yellow Pages. You can get much of this industry data by doing library research. See Chapter 5, No-Cost Market Research, for more on library research.

Options are available to help your business develop an effective advertising budget and guidelines. Research, practice, and feedback on sales effectiveness will help you build your marketing mastery over time.

Worksheet 29 – Your Advertising Budget Worksheet

Your advertising budget should be comparable to industry standards and to what your chief competitors are spending. This worksheet will help you assess your industry's expenditures on advertising and to adjust your own advertising spending accordingly.

How much did you spend last year on advertising, if you were in business? $ _____

Sales were: $ _____

Calculate advertising as a percent of sales for last year. $= \dfrac{\text{Advertising Costs}}{\text{Total Sales}} =$ _____%

Were you satisfied with the return on advertising expenses?   Yes ☐ No ☐

What way do you have of measuring effectiveness of your advertising? _____

_____

Do your major competitors spend more or less than you do on advertising? _____

Your sales goals for next year are what percentage of last year? _____%

This translates to a goal of $ _____

Using national percentage of sales figures for your industry, how much would you budget for next year's advertising? _____

_____

What are industry averages as a percentage of sales? _____

Do other businesses in your industry allocate a fixed amount to advertising each month?   Yes ☐ No ☐

List positive or negative social, political, demographic, psychological, economic, or legal factors that might affect sales next year. _____

_____

_____

How might current business trends affect sales? _____

Based on all the above indicators, next year's advertising budget will need to be: $ _____ total spent, or an average of $ _____ per month to reach your sales goal.

What cooperative advertising possibilities are available and how much will they cost? _____

_____

If you want to include in your budget the cost of an advertising agency or media consultant, how much are you willing to spend? $ _____

Worksheet 30 – Yearly Sales Forecast and Marketing Budget

	January Budget	January Actual	February Budget	February Actual	March Budget	March Actual	April Budget	April Actual	May Budget	May Actual
Sales										
Marketing Budget										
Advertising: Television										
Radio										
Newspapers										
Magazines										
Yellow Pages										
Printed Materials: Direct Mail										
Flyers/Brochures										
Coupons										
Posters/Handbills										
Catalogs										
Newsletter										
Other Printed Materials										
Signs and Displays: Billboard/Transit										
Point-of-Purchase/ Windows										
Sales Promotion										
Publicity and Public Relations										
Personal Selling and Sales Training										
Other Marketing Ideas:										

Worksheet 30 – Yearly Sales Forecast and Marketing Budget (continued)

June		July		August		September		October		November		December	
Budget	Actual	Budget	Actual	Budget	Actual	Budget	Actual	Budget	Actual	Budget	Actual	Budget	Actual

20 | Explore International Markets

Once you understand how to run a successful operation locally and are ready to expand, you may find new customers in other cities, states, provinces, regions, or countries. Even in the initial planning stages of going into business, you may want to explore national and international markets as your ultimate goal. Your initial market research done in Step 2 can help you decide if international activity is a viable focus for your business from the beginning, or better reserved for an expansion move later on.

The global economy of the twenty-first century presents an opportunity to small business unknown before. For many entrepreneurs, international marketing is a necessity; however, understanding domestic marketing, before getting into the international arena, normally takes two to five years. This book focuses on how to get through those first few years. Nonetheless, you may want to consider the international market for your products, and this chapter will help you plan ahead.

Researching the Global Market

One of the major deterrents to owners and managers of small businesses interested in entering foreign trade markets has been the lack of a simple procedure to obtain information. As an exporter, you will want to research contact points, organizational facilities, promotional activities, documentation, and many other questions.

Several agencies of the federal government can now furnish information on exporting, importing, economics and marketing, financing opportunities, documentation requirements, customs, regulations, transportation facilities, and other related topics. Among these agencies are the Overseas Private Investment Corporation (OPIC), the Agency for International Development (AID), and the Small Business Administration (SBA). In addition, the United Nations and the World Bank send missions and study teams to prepare reports on economic, political, and social conditions in most trading nations of the world. The Export-Import Bank maintains a special office to provide information and service, discount loans, and foreign bank credits to small exporters. The SBA provides information through its Management Assistance Program to potential small business or minority exporters.

Export workshops and training programs are cosponsored by SBA District Offices with the Commerce Department and others interested in international trade. The SBA's Small Business Development Centers (SBDCs) offer export counseling in more than 700 locations in the United States.

The U.S. Department of Commerce has several export programs at more than 68 district offices. They have trade counselors to provide export advice and computerized market data on more than 150 locations, plus contacts in many countries.

You can evaluate market potential, growth, and risk through published resources. For example, Business International publishes information on three indices for countries in Western and Eastern Europe, the Middle East, Latin American, Asia, Africa, and Australia. They look at market growth, market intensity, and market size. The specific variables included in each of these indices vary somewhat from region to region, reflecting different market characteristics.

The U.S. Department of Commerce publishes detailed global market surveys covering the best foreign markets for a given industry, such as graphics, industrial or medical equipment, and computers. The reports provide an easily accessible, predigested survey of world markets. You can select attractive market prospects by matching a specific product range with a company's competitive advantage in supplying that market.

Conducting Business Internationally

Besides obtaining general information on exports of various products, you need to have a basic knowledge of the country in which your business plans to operate. This is no easy task for an outsider. It usually takes several years just to figure out how to successfully conduct business in a foreign country.

Some of the questions you will need to answer before you begin doing business with another country include:

- What are the business and social customs, the common courtesies you should observe? For example, consider how to greet people, give gifts, or pay for business lunches. How long is the normal working day? What are some dominant business values? Should you be on time or late for a meeting?

- What is the social structure? What are important class and ethnic divisions? Is consensus valued more than individuality? Are Americans liked or disliked, and for what reasons? What is your attitude toward the society?

- Which laws are most important for you to know? What is the economic and political environment?

Global expansion takes planning and trial and error. You need to assess whether exporting is the best option for you, or whether you should license, franchise, establish a joint venture, barter, establish an international location, or use an export middleperson. You must deal with the issues of insurance and financing. Base all of these decisions on a foundation of serious market research, and develop a business plan for your international expansion.

Deciding to Go Global

Whether you have been in business for several years or are just starting out, you can look at several particular aspects of your business to see if it is suited for international operations. Worksheet 31, International Marketing Checklist, at the end of this chapter will help you decide how many of the key indicators you have for launching a successful international marketing campaign.

A stagnant domestic market is one key indicator that your business should consider the international arena. For example, if you manufacture traditional file drawers, and you do not plan to change your product line, the trend in the United States to computers may decrease the need for traditional file cabinets. However, a developing country would be a natural market for them. You could market to businesses or individuals in countries that have not yet adopted widespread use of computer technology and that still rely on paper to store information.

If your business does not use its productive capacity to the fullest, you might consider expanding your market internationally. For example, if a computer is used only 25% of the time, machines go unused for several hours, or employees are on involuntary part-time or short workweek schedules, you could produce more if you found new markets or licensed other businesses to use your excess capacity. If you can expand your market internationally without having to make a big capital outlay — without having to buy extra equipment or hire additional personnel — exploring the possibility is certainly worthwhile.

You might also investigate whether you could enjoy tax or customs advantages to exporting. For example, some businesses can get a refund of customs duty for some materials. Several free trade zones are now in operation in many countries that might allow you tariff-free trade. If you import goods for processing, assembly, and re-exporting, you may not have to pay duties or federal excise tax. Ask your attorney or accountant what kinds of tax or tariff benefits your business might enjoy and in which trade zones.

Some countries require that businesses make modifications to their products to meet certain safety, environmental, or other types of regulations before they allow the products to be imported. However, if you can find countries, or at least one specific country, that does not require you to make any modifications to your product, you might consider marketing and selling your product there.

Finally, a very important consideration before deciding to export, and one that could save you many problems in the short and long term, is whether you have contacts in other countries who could serve as partners, distributors, or manufactures. Having a trusted person who knows the cultural ins and outs, legalities, and politics of doing business in another country is critical. Building a sales or production system from scratch can be a long, arduous process, even if you know the language, customs, politics, and markets. You need to build networks. If you have contacts inside the country who can help you build these vital networks, the possibility of launching a successful international marketing campaign is far greater than without them.

International Markets Summary

The international scene is changing rapidly. Before you plan for international marketing, first understand marketing in your domestic scene. Then, if you are in the United States, go to an SBA Information Center, Small Business Development Center, or U.S. Department of Commerce office for further information. You can also consult several good books on exporting, including The Oasis Press' *Export Now: A Guide for Small Business.*

Marketing is a process that is customer-focused. If you follow the seven step marketing process described in this book, you will be ahead of your competitors in preparing for every marketing concern. You will secure satisfied-plus customers and watch your sales grow. Reuse and reapply the ideas and worksheets in this book each time you reassess your marketing campaign. If you do, you will design a successful, personalized marketing strategy and be well on your way to marketing mastery.

Worksheet 31 – International Marketing Checklist

Answering yes to any of the following questions may indicate that you should explore global possibilities to expand or redefine your target market or add new customers.

Yes   No

☐   ☐   Is your domestic market stagnant?

☐   ☐   Is the level of economic activity in your industry peaking?

☐   ☐   Do you have excess productive capacity?

☐   ☐   Are there some possible tax advantages from importing certain materials and components that could be used in products to be exported?

☐   ☐   Are there other countries, or at least one specific one, in which your product or service could be sold with little or no modifications?

☐   ☐   Are you aware from your travels or information from other sources of certain products or services that might be appropriate for a foreign market?

☐   ☐   Do you have one or several contacts in other countries who might make good partners, distributors, or manufacturers?

☐   ☐   Are there certain processes in the manufacture or assembly of your product that could be accomplished more cheaply or with higher quality elsewhere?

☐   ☐   Have you received inquiries for your products from other countries?

☐   ☐   Are there fluctuations in annual workload that could be offset by demand in another country?

☐   ☐   Do you have excess liquidity that might be able to get increased return in the international arena?

☐   ☐   Do you or any of your employees have special skills or knowledge of another country that you could capitalize on?

☐   ☐   Do you know of a local expert on the country you are considering?

Index

Remember Those Who Have Made Your Business A $uccess

... And They Will Remember You!

Whether you operate as a corporation of 500 employees or a sole proprietorship, your customers are more valuable to you than ever before. When did you last take the time to personally thank those individuals who have contributed to the success of your business?

- Do your customers know that you appreciate them?

- Do they know that their business problems are a concern to you?

- Do they know you will keep them up to date on special offerings and new products?

"In sales work, we are always looking for every possible "edge" to communicate and convince customers we're different and better. EXECARDS helps do both of these things extremely well... I know 98% of most competitors don't use them. I consider this my advantage."

Jim Moonan, Principal Director and Sales Trainer
Educational/Training Services Bureau

What better way to do this than by using EXECARDS® the original business-to-business communication cards.

Fast friendly, and direct, EXECARDS are a welcome change from the standard business letter or endless rounds of telephone tag. With prices starting at $.39 EXECARDS will make your marketing effort possible on even the smallest budget.

For a free color brochure call 1-800-228-2275

Mention this ad to receive a 10% discount on your first order of EXECARDS

PSI Research/EXECARDS 300 North Valley Drive, Grants Pass, OR 97526 ☎(503) 479-9464 FAX (503) 476-1479

Get business tips from over 157 seasoned experts.

Business Formation and Planning

Start Your Business:
A Beginner's Guide

Book

This handy, easy-to-read book is full of checklists to help answer your start-up questions. Helps you ask the right questions and find out where you can get the answers. The Plan of Action Worksheets make it easy to compile and coordinate your to-do list. The book is divided into sections covering business, legal, marketing, human resources, sales, taxes, and other decisions.

The Successful Business
Plan: Secrets & Strategies

Book and software
for IBM & compatibles

Start-to-finish guide on creating a successful business plan. Includes tips from venture capitalists, bankers, and successful CEOs. Features worksheets for ease in planning and budgeting with the Abrams Method of Flow-Through Financials. Gives a sample business plan, plus specialized help for retailers, service companies, manufacturers, and in-house corporate plans. Also tells how to find funding sources.

Starting and Operating a
Business in... series
Available for each state plus District of
Columbia

Newly
Updated

One-stop resource to current federal and state laws and regulations that affect businesses. Clear "human language" explanations of complex issues, plus samples of government forms, and sources for additional help or information. Helps seasoned business owners keep up with changing legislation, and guides new entrepreneurs step-by-step to start and run the business. Includes many checklists and worksheets to organize ideas, create action plans, and project financial scenarios.

The Essential Corporation
Handbook

Book   *Newly*
Updated

This comprehensive reference for small business corporations in all 50 states and Washington, D.C. explains the legal requirements for maintaining a corporation in good standing. Features many sample corporate documents which are annotated by the author to show what to look for and what to look out for. Tells how to avoid personal liability as an officer, director, or shareholder.

Surviving and Prospering
in a Business Partnership

Book

From evaluation of potential partners, through the drafting of agreements, to day-to-day management of working relationships, this book helps avoid classic partnership catastrophes. Discusses how to set up the partnership to reduce the financial and emotional consequences of unanticipated disputes, dishonesty, divorce, disability, or death of a partner.

California Corporation
Formation Package and
Minute Book

Book and software
for IBM & Mac

Provides forms required for incorporating and maintaining closely held corporations, including: articles of incorporation; bylaws; stock certificates, stock transfer record sheets, bill of sale agreement; minutes form; plus many others. Addresses questions on fees, timing, notices, regulations, election of directors and other critical factors. Software has minutes, bylaws, and articles of incorporation already for you to edit and customize (using your own word processor).

Franchise Bible:
A Comprehensive Guide

Book
Newly
Updated

Complete guide to franchising for prospective franchisees or for business owners considering franchising their business. Includes actual sample documents, such as a complete offering circular, plus worksheets for evaluating franchise companies, locations, and organizing information before seeing an attorney. This book is helpful for lawyers as well as their clients.

Home Business Made Easy

Book

Thinking of starting a business at home? This book is the easiest road to starting a home business. Shows you how to select and start a home business that fits your interests, lifestyle and pocketbook. Walks you through 153 different businesses you could operate from home full or part time. Author David Hanania has boiled the process down to simple steps so you can get started now to realize your dreams.

The Small Business Expert
Software for IBM-PC & compatibles

Newly
Updated

Generates comprehensive custom checklist of the state and federal laws and regulations based on your type and size of business. Allows comparison of doing business in each of the 50 states. Built-in worksheets create outlines for personnel policies, marketing feasibility studies, and a business plan draft. *Requires 256K RAM and hard disk.*

Starting and Operating a
Business: U.S. Edition
Set of eleven
binders   *Newly*
Updated

The complete encyclopedia of how to do business in the U.S. Describes laws and regulations for each state, plus Washington, D.C., as well as the federal government. Includes lists of sources of help, plus post cards for requesting materials from government agencies. This set is valuable for businesses with locations or marketing activities in several states, plus franchisors, attorneys, and other consultants.

To order these business tools, use the enclosed order form, FAX 503-476-1479 or call us toll-free at 800-228-2275

Step-by-step techniques for generating more profit.

Financial Management

Top Tax Saving Ideas for Today's Small Business

New Book

Newly Updated

An extensive summary of every imaginable tax break that is still available in today's "reformed" tax environment. Deals with the various entities that the owner/manager may choose to operate a business. Identifies a wide assortment of tax deduction, fringe benefits, and tax deferrals. Includes a simplified checklist of recent tax law changes with an emphasis on tax breaks.

Financial Management Techniques for Small Business

Book and software for IBM-PC & compatibles

Clearly reveals the essential ingredients of sound financial management in detail. By monitoring trends in your financial activities, you will be able to uncover potential problems before they become crises. You'll understand why you can be making a profit and still not have the cash to meet expenses, and you'll learn the steps to change your business' cash behavior to get more return for your effort. Software makes your business' financial picture graphically clear, and lets you look at "what if" scenarios.

The Buyer's Guide to Business Insurance

Book and software for IBM-PC & compatibles

New!

Straightforward advice on shopping for insurance, understanding types of coverage, comparing proposals and premium rates. Worksheets help identify and weigh the risks a particular business is likely to face, then determine if any of those might be safely self-insured or eliminated. Request for proposal form helps businesses avoid over-paying for protection. Software guides you through process of completing multiple forms and editing letters.

Collection Techniques for Small Business

Book

Newly Updated

Practical tips on how to turn receivables into cash. Worksheets and checklists help businesses establish credit policies, track accounts, and flag when it is necessary to bring in a collection agency, attorney, or go to court. This book advises how to deal with disputes, negotiate settlements, win in small claims court, and collect on judgments. Gives examples of telephone collection techniques and collection letters.

Secrets to Buying and Selling a Business

New Book

New!

Prepares a business buyer or seller for negotiations that will achieve win-win results. Shows how to determine the real worth of a business, including intangible assets such as "goodwill." Over 36 checklists and worksheets on topics such as tax impact on buyers and sellers, escrow checklist, cash flow projections, evaluating potential buyers, financing options, and many others.

Business Owner's Guide to Accounting & Bookkeeping

Book

Makes understanding the economics of business simple. Explains the basic accounting principles that relate to any business. Step-by-step instructions for generating accounting statements and interpreting them, spotting errors, and recognizing warning signs. Discusses how banks and other creditors view financial statements.

Bottom Line Basics

Book

New!

Guides you past the mechanics of accounting to an understanding of how financial management helps meet your business goals. Provides a ten step plan of attack to immediately improve cash flow, reduce costs, and give a better understanding of the numbers driving your business.

Financial Templates

Software for IBM-PC & Mac

Calculates and graphs many business "what-if" scenarios and financial reports. Twenty-eight financial templates such as income statements, cash flow, and balance sheet comparisons, break-even analyses, product contribution comparisons, market share, net present value, sales model, pro formas, loan payment projections, etc. *Requires Lotus 1-2-3, Microsoft Excel 2.0 or higher for IBM. Microsoft Excel 4.0 or higher for MAC.*

Yes, we accept credit cards — VISA, MasterCard, American Express, Discover, or your personal or business check.

Proven tools and ideas to expand your business.

Marketing & Public Relations

Power Marketing

Book

A wealth of basic, how-to marketing information that easily takes a new or experienced business owner through the essentials of marketing and sales strategies, customer database marketing, advertising, public relations, budgeting, and follow-up marketing systems. Written in a friendly tone by a marketing educator, the book features worksheets with step-by-step instructions, a glossary of marketing terms, and a sample marketing plan. Also available: *Power Marketing Tools for Small Business*—two hours of audio tapes by author Jody Hornor that reveal 81 tools you can use to increase your market power.

How To Develop & Market Creative Business Ideas

Book

Step-by-step manual guides the inventor through all stages of new product development. Discusses patenting your invention, trademarks, copyrights, and how to construct your prototype. Gives information on financing, distribution, test marketing, and finding licensees. Plus, lists many useful sources for prototype resources, trade shows, funding, and more.

Know Your Market: How to do Low Cost Market Research

Book **Newly Updated**

Workbook explains how a small business can conduct its own market research. Shows how to set objectives, determine which techniques to use, create a schedule, and then monitor expenses. Encompasses primary research (trade shows, telephone interviews, mail surveys), plus secondary research (using available information in print).

Marketing Mastery

Book **New!**

Consider how you can capitalize at every opportunity the customers' feeling of satisfaction with your product and your business. Thirty worksheets help you apply the marketing process to your own business. Marketing is presented in a seven step process that will help you acquire and keep satisfied customers.

International Business

Export Now

Book

Prepares a business to enter the export market. Clearly explains the basics, then articulates specific requirements for export licensing, preparation of documents, payment methods, packaging, and shipping. Includes advice on evaluating foreign representatives, planning international marketing strategies, and discovering official U.S. policy for various countries and regions. Lists sources.

Now – Find Out How Your Business Can Profit By Being Environmentally Aware

The Business Environmental Handbook

Book

Save your business while you are saving the planet. Here's your chance to learn about the hundreds of ways any business can help secure its future by starting to conserve resources now. This book reveals little-understood but simple techniques for recycling, precycling, and conservation that can save your business money now, and help preserve resources. Also gives tips on "green marketing" to customers .

Give yourself and your business every chance to succeed. Order the business tools you need today. Call 800-228-2275.

Gain the power of increased knowledge — Oasis is your source.

Acquiring Outside Capital

Raising Capital: How to Write a Financing Proposal

New Book

Valuable resource for writing and presenting a winning loan proposal. Includes professional tips on how to write the proposal. Presents detailed examples of the four most common types of proposals to secure venture capital and loans: Private Placement Circular; Prospectus or Public Offering; Financing Proposal; and Limited Partnership Offering.

The Money Connection: Where & How to Apply for Business Loans

New Book

Comprehensive listing of funding sources. Lists hundreds of current nationally recognized business loan and venture capital firms. Describes the latest federal, state, county, and community loan, investment and assistance programs. Gives addresses and phone numbers of federal agency offices in each state.

Financing Your Small Business

Book

Essential techniques to successfully identify, approach, attract, and manage sources of financing. Shows how to gain the full benefits of debt financing while minimizing its risks. Outlines all types of financing and walks you step by step through the process, from evaluating short-term credit options, through negotiating a long-term loan, to deciding whether to go public.

The Loan Package

Book

Preparatory package for a business loan proposal. Worksheets help analyze cash needs and articulate business focus. Includes sample forms for balance sheets, income statements, projections, and budget reports. Screening sheets rank potential lenders to shorten the time involved in getting the loan.

The Successful Business Plan: Secrets & Strategies

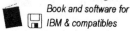
Book and software for IBM & compatibles

Now you can find out what venture capitalists and bankers really want to see before they will fund a company. This book gives you their personal tips and insights. The Abrams Method of Flow-Through Financials breaks down the chore into easy to manage steps, so you can end up with a fundable proposal. Software is available for this book—see the back page of this catalog or call 1-800-228-2275 for a free software catalog. *Software requires a hard drive.*

Financial Templates
Software for IBM & compatibles & Mac

Software speeds business calculations. Includes 28 financial templates including various projections, statements, ratios, histories, amortizations, and cash flows. This is just one of many useful software packages designed specifically for small businesses. Call 1-800-228-2275 for information. *Requires Lotus 1-2-3, Microsoft Excel 2.0 or higher for IBM. Microsoft Excel 4.0 or higher for MAC.*

Human Resource Ideas

A Company Policy and Personnel Workbook

Book and software for IBM & compatibles

Saves costly consultant or staff hours in creating company personnel policies. Provides model policies on topics such as employee safety, leave of absence, flextime, smoking, substance abuse, sexual harassment, performance improvement, grievance procedure. For each subject, practical and legal ramifications are explained, then a choice of alternate policies presented. Software is available for this book. Check our software catalog or call 1-800-228-2275 for more information.

People Investment

Book

Written for the business owner or manager who is not a personnel specialist. Explains what you must know to make your hiring decisions pay off for everyone. Learn more about the Americans With Disabilities Act (ADA), Medical and Family Leave, and more.

Managing People: A Practical Guide

Book

Focuses on developing the art of working with people to maximize the productivity and satisfaction of both manager and employees. Discussions, exercises, and self-tests boost skills in communicating, delegating, motivating, developing teams, goal-setting, adapting to change, and coping with stress.

Safety Law Compliance Manual for California Businesses

Book

Now every California employer must have an Injury and Illness Prevention Program that meets the specific requirements of Senate Bill 198. Already, thousands of citations have been issued to companies who did not comply with all seven components of the complicated new law. Avoid fines by using this guide to set up a program that will meet Cal/OSHA standards. Includes forms.

Plus optional binder for your company's safety program

Also available — Company Injury and Illness Prevention Program Binder — Pre-organized and ready-to-use with forms, tabs, logs and sample documents. Saves your company time, work, and worry.

Why hesitate? If any product you order doesn't meet your needs, just return it for full refund or credit. 800-228-2275.

Unique cards get you noticed. Books & software save you time.

Business Communications

Proposal Development: How to Respond and Win the Bid

Book

Orchestrates a successful proposal from preliminary planning to clinching the deal. Shows by explanation and example how to: determine what to include; create text, illustrations, tables, exhibits, and appendices; how to format (using either traditional methods or desktop publishing); meet the special requirements of government proposals; set up and follow a schedule.

Write Your Own Business Contracts

Book

Explains the "do's" and "don'ts" of contract writing so any person in business can do the preparatory work in drafting contracts before hiring an attorney for final review. Gives a working knowledge of the various types of business agreements, plus tips on how to prepare for the unexpected.

Complete Book of Business Forms

Book

Over 200 reproducible forms for all types of business needs: personnel, employment, finance, production flow, operations, sales, marketing, order entry, and general administration. Time-saving, uniform, coordinated way to record and locate important business information.

EXECARDS®
Business-To-Business Communication Cards Portfolio Assortments 12 cards with envelopes $12.95 ea.

Prepare yourself for those occasions that sneak up on you at a moment's notice with quality, business greeting cards. Order EXECARDS Portfolios in handsome folders of granite-textured cover stock that fit handily in your file drawer. Five assortments are available: Happy Birthday/AS61, Personal Greetings/AS62, Thank You/AS63, Marketing/AS68, and Follow Up/AS69. To see the complete EXECARDS line, call 1-800-228-2275 for your free color brochure.

Business Relocation

Company Relocation Handbook: Making the Right Move

Book

Comprehensive guide to moving a business. Begins with defining objectives for moving and evaluating whether relocating will actually solve more problems than it creates. Worksheets compare prospective locations, using rating scales for physical plant, equipment, personnel, and geographic considerations. Sets up a schedule for dealing with logistics.

Retirement Planning

Secure Your Future

Book **Newly Updated**

Do-it-yourself workbook for setting up a retirement plan that can easily be maintained and followed. Covers establishing net worth, retirement goals, budgets, and a plan for asset acquisition, preservation, and growth. Discusses realistic expectations for Social Security, Medicare, and health care alternatives. Features special sections for business owners.

Mail Order

Mail Order Legal Guide

New Book

For companies that use the mail to market their products or services, as well as for mail order businesses, this book clarifies complex regulations so penalties can be avoided. Gives state-by-state legal requirements, plus information on Federal Trade Commission guidelines and rules covering

How Do People *Feel* about Your Company?

Control Your Company's *Finances!*

Templates for Your Business Needs!

Break-Even Analysis

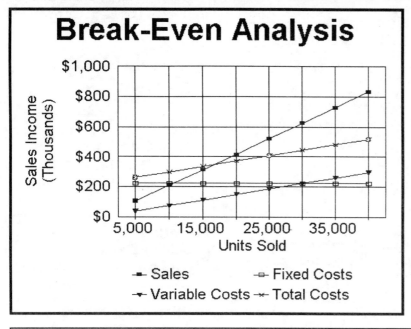

- ■ Sales
- ▼ Variable Costs
- □ Fixed Costs
- ✳ Total Costs

Financial Templates

for Small Business
(for Lotus 1-2-3 & Microsoft Excel)

- ◆ Income Statement: Ann. by Month (History)
- ◆ Cash Flow: Ann. by Month (Historical)
- ◆ Current Financial Situation: by Month
- ◆ Statement of Cash Flows
- ◆ Balance Sheet
- ◆ Staffing Chart
- ◆ Income Statement: Annual by Month
- ◆ Income Statement: Annual for 5 Years
- ◆ Monthly Sales Projections
- ◆ Monthly Cash Income Projections

- ◆ Cash-Flow Projections: Annual by Month
- ◆ Personal Financial Statement
- ◆ Forecast vs. Actual Income Statement and Cash Flow comparison
- ◆ Forecast vs. Actual Balance Sheet
- ◆ Financial Ratio Analysis
- ◆ Break-even Analysis
- ◆ Capital Needed to Purchase a Business
- ◆ Net Present Value Worksheet
- ◆ Competitive Analysis: Customer Perception

- and Internal Operations
- ◆ Market Share Distribution
- ◆ Tangible Assets Worksheet
- ◆ Production Control & Cost Sheet
- ◆ Normalized Profit & Loss (Income) Statement
- ◆ Contribution Margin by Product/Product Line
- ◆ Internal Rate of Return Analysis
- ◆ Adjustable Rate Loan: Fixed Payment
- ◆ Fixed Rate Loan: Amortized to End of Loan
- ◆ Adjustable Rate Loan: Variable Payment

Multipurpose Templates for Your Business

PSI Research/The Oasis Press has reworked these valuable business tools to make it even easier for you to evaluate the financial position of your business.

Financial Templates for Small Business includes 28 templates which cover everything from Annual Income to Variable Rate Loan Amortization, and the manual shows you how and where to use them in simple terms.

There are historical spreadsheets to help you analyze historical information, forecast spreadsheets to help you predict the future and a variety of other spreadsheets to aid you in evaluating your business and the proposed purchase of another's business. Whether your business is existing or not, these templates will help you plan for the future.

These new *Financial Templates for Small Business* are sure to make an impact on the way you keep track of your business resources and will make a valuable addition to your business computer library.

System Requirements:
    IBM or compatible computer
    Lotus 1-2-3 release 1A or higher,
    Microsoft Excel v 2,
    Quattro Pro, or
    Any truly compatible spreadsheet program

Market Share Analysis
% of Revenue

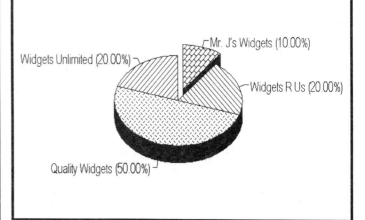

- Widgets Unlimited (20.00%)
- Mr. J's Widgets (10.00%)
- Widgets R Us (20.00%)
- Quality Widgets (50.00%)

Ordering Information...800-228-2275

FTMPSTMP3I   *Financial Templates* for IBM $ 69.95

*Financial Templates for Small Business includes one 3.5" disk and instruction manual. You may choose to install Lotus or Microsoft Excel format, or choose to install both.

BOOKS FROM THE OASIS PRESS® Please check the edition (binder or paperback) of your choice

TITLE	BINDER	PAPERBACK	QUANTITY	COST
Bottom Line Basics	☐ $ 39.95	☐ $ 19.95		
The Business Environmental Handbook		☐ $ 19.95		
Business Owner's Guide to Accounting & Bookkeeping		☐ $ 19.95		
Buyer's Guide to Business Insurance	☐ $ 39.95	☐ $ 19.95		
California Corporation Formation Package and Minute Book	☐ $ 39.95	☐ $ 29.95		
Collection Techniques for Small Business	☐ $ 39.95	☐ $ 19.95		
A Company Policy and Personnel Workbook	☐ $ 49.95	☐ $ 29.95		
Company Relocation Handbook	☐ $ 39.95	☐ $ 19.95		
Complete Book of Business Forms	☐ $ 49.95	☐ $ 19.95		
The Essential Corporation Handbook		☐ $ 19.95		
Export Now	☐ $ 39.95	☐ $ 19.95		
Financial Management Techniques For Small Business	☐ $ 39.95	☐ $ 19.95		
Financing Your Small Business		☐ $ 19.95		
Franchise Bible	☐ $ 39.95	☐ $ 19.95		
Home Business Made Easy		☐ $ 19.95		
How to Develop & Market Creative Business Ideas		☐ $ 14.95		
Know Your Market: How To Do Low Cost Market Research	☐ $ 39.95	☐ $ 19.95		
The Loan Package	☐ $ 39.95			
Mail Order Legal Guide	☐ $ 45.00	☐ $ 29.95		
Managing People: A Practical Guide	☐ $ 39.95	☐ $ 19.95		
Marketing Mastery	☐ $ 39.95	☐ $ 19.95		
The Money Connection	☐ $ 39.95	☐ $ 19.95		
People Investment	☐ $ 39.95	☐ $ 19.95		
Power Marketing for Small Business	☐ $ 39.95	☐ $ 19.95		
Proposal Development: How to Respond and Win the Bid (hardback book)	☐ $ 39.95	☐ $ 19.95		
Raising Capital	☐ $ 39.95	☐ $ 19.95		
Safety Law Compliance Manual for California Businesses	☐ $ 39.95	☐ $ 24.95		
Company Illness & Injury Prevention Program Binder (OR Get kit WITH BOOK AND binder $49.95)	☐ $ 34.95	☐ $ 49.95 BOOK & BINDER KIT		
Secrets to Buying and Selling a Business	☐ $ 39.95	☐ $ 19.95		
Secure Your Future: Financial Planning at Any Age	☐ $ 39.95	☐ $ 19.95		
Start Your Business		☐ $ 8.95		
Starting and Operating A Business in... book INCLUDES FEDERAL section PLUS ONE STATE SECTION —	☐ $ 29.95	☐ $ 24.95		
PLEASE SPECIFY WHICH STATE(S) YOU WANT:				
STATE SECTION ONLY (BINDER NOT INCLUDED) – SPECIFY STATES:	☐ $ 8.95			
U.S. EDITION (FEDERAL SECTION – 50 STATES AND WASHINGTON, D.C. IN 11-BINDER SET)	☐ $295.00			
Successful Business Plan: Secrets & Strategies (GET THE BINDER...IT'S A BUSINESS PLAN KIT)	☐ $ 49.95	☐ $ 21.95		
Surviving and Prospering in a Business Partnership	☐ $ 39.95	☐ $ 19.95		
Top Tax Saving Ideas for Today's Small Business		☐ $ 14.95		
Write Your Own Business Contracts (HARDBACK BOOK)	☐ $ 39.95	☐ $ 19.95		

SOFTWARE Please check whether you use Macintosh or 3-1/2" Disk for IBM-PC & Compatibles

TITLE	3-1/2" IBM Disk	Mac	Price	QUANTITY	COST
California Corporation Formation Package Software	☐	☐	$ 39.95		
H California Corporation Formation Binder book & Software	☐	☐	$ 69.95		
Company Policy & Personnel Software (Standalone)	☐		$ 99.95		
H Company Policy & Personnel Binder book & Software (Standalone)	☐		$125.95		
Financial Management Techniques	☐		$ 99.95		
H Financial Management Techniques Binder book & Software	☐		$129.95		
Financial Templates	☐	☐	$ 69.95		
The Small Business Expert	☐		$ 34.95		
Successful Business Plan (Full Standalone)	☐		$ 99.95		
H Successful Business Plan Binder book & Software (Full Standalone)	☐		$125.95		
SOFTWARE TOTAL (Please enter on other side also for grand total)					

Please add above totals on other side to complete your order. Thanks!

PSI Successful Business Library / Tools for Business Success Order Form (please see other side also)
Call, Mail or Fax to: PSI Research, 300 North Valley Drive, Grants Pass, OR 97526 USA
Order Phone USA (800) 228-2275   Inquiries and International Orders (503) 479-9464   FAX (503) 476-1479

New titles coming to you from *The Oasis Press* in 1995.

Title	Pub.	Binder	Paperback	Qunatity	Cost
A Firm Foundation: How To Secure Venture Capital	March	☐ $ 39.95	☐ $ 19.95		
Customer Engineering: Cutting Edge Selling Strategies	April	☐ $ 39.95	☐ $ 19.95		
Marketing Mastery: Your Seven Step Guide to Success	April	☐ $ 39.95	☐ $ 19.95		
Doing Business in Russia	May		☐ $ 19.95		
The Money Connection: Where and How to Apply for Business Loans/ Venture Capital	May	☐ $ 39.95	☐ $ 19.95		
Successful Network Marketing for The 21st Century	May	☐ $ 39.95	☐ $ 19.95		
The Essential Limited Liability Company Handbook	June	☐ $ 39.95	☐ $ 19.95		
Funding for Women, Minorities and Disabled Entrepreneurs	July	☐ $ 39.95	☐ $ 19.95		
Legal Expense Defense: How to Control Your Business' Legal Costs and Problems	July	☐ $ 39.95	☐ $ 19.95		
Comp Control: The Secrets of Reducing Workers' Compensation Costs	July	☐ $ 39.95	☐ $ 19.95		

Place your order before publication date and get a 20% discount off of the regular price. Your credit card will not be billed until the day the book is shipped.

Sold to: PLEASE GIVE STREET ADDRESS NOT P.O. BOX FOR SHIPPING

Name _____   Title: _____

Company _____   Daytime Telephone: _____

Street Address _____

City/State/Zip _____

☐   *YES, I want to receive the PSI newsletter, ¹MEMO.*
      Be sure to include: Name, address, and telephone number above.

Ship to: (if different) PLEASE GIVE STREET ADDRESS NOT P.O. BOX FOR SHIPPING

Name _____

Title _____

Company _____

Street Address _____

City/State/Zip _____

Daytime Telephone _____

Payment Information:

☐ Check enclosed payable to PSI Research (When you enclose a check, UPS ground shipping is free within the Continental U.S.A.)

Charge - ☐ VISA ☐ MASTERCARD ☐ AMEX ☐ DISCOVER   Card Number: _____ Expires _____

Signature: _____   Name on card: _____

EXECARDS — The Personal Business Communications Tool

ITEM	PRICE	QUANTITY	COST

TOTAL (Please enter also for grand total) $ _____

Many additional options available, including custom imprinting of your company's name, logo or message. Please request a complete catalog. 800-228-2275

Please send me:

_____ EXECARDS Catalog

_____ Oasis Press Software Information

_____ Oasis Press Book Information

YOUR GRAND TOTAL

BOOK TOTAL (from other side)	$
BOOK TOTAL (1995 Titles)	$
SOFTWARE TOTAL (from other side)	$
EXECARDS TOTAL	$
TOTAL ORDER	$

Rush service is available. Please call us for details.

Use this form to register for advance notification of updates, new books and software releases, plus special customer discounts!

Please answer these questions to let us know how our products are working for you, and what we could do to serve you better.

Title of book or software purchased from us: _____

It is a:
- ☐ Binder book
- ☐ Paperback book
- ☐ Book/software combination
- ☐ Software only

Rate this product's overall quality of information:
- ☐ Excellent
- ☐ Good
- ☐ Fair
- ☐ Poor

Rate the quality of printed materials:
- ☐ Excellent
- ☐ Good
- ☐ Fair
- ☐ Poor

Rate the format:
- ☐ Excellent
- ☐ Good
- ☐ Fair
- ☐ Poor

Did the product provide what you needed?
- ☐ Yes ☐ No

If not, what should be added? _____
_____
_____
_____
_____

This product is:
- ☐ Clear and easy to follow
- ☐ Too complicated
- ☐ Too elementary

Were the worksheets (if any) easy to use?
- ☐ Yes ☐ No ☐ N/A

Should we include:
- ☐ More worksheets
- ☐ Fewer worksheets
- ☐ No worksheets

How do you feel about the price?
- ☐ Lower than expected
- ☐ About right
- ☐ Too expensive

How many employees are in your company?
- ☐ Under 10 employees
- ☐ 10 – 50 employees
- ☐ 51 – 99 employees
- ☐ 100 – 250 employees
- ☐ Over 250 employees

How many people in the city your company is in?
- ☐ 50,000 – 100,000
- ☐ 100,000 – 500,000
- ☐ 500,000 – 1,000,000
- ☐ Over 1,000,000
- ☐ Rural (under 50,000)

What is your type of business?
- ☐ Retail
- ☐ Service
- ☐ Government
- ☐ Manufacturing
- ☐ Distributor
- ☐ Education

What types of products or services do you sell?
_____
_____
_____
_____

What is your position in the company?
(please check one)
- ☐ Owner
- ☐ Administration
- ☐ Sales/marketing
- ☐ Finance
- ☐ Human resources
- ☐ Production
- ☐ Operations
- ☐ Computer/MIS

How did you learn about this product?
- ☐ Recommended by a friend
- ☐ Used in a seminar or class
- ☐ Have used other PSI products
- ☐ Received a mailing
- ☐ Saw in bookstore
- ☐ Saw in library
- ☐ Saw review in:
  - ☐ Newspaper
  - ☐ Magazine
  - ☐ TV/Radio

Where did you buy this product?
- ☐ Catalog
- ☐ Bookstore
- ☐ Office supply
- ☐ Consultant
- ☐ Other_____

Would you purchase other business tools from us?
- ☐ Yes ☐ No

If so, which products interest you?
- ☐ EXECARDS® Communication Tools
- ☐ Books for business
- ☐ Software

Would you recommend this product to a friend?
- ☐ Yes ☐ No

If you'd like us to send associates or friends a catalog, just list names and addresses on back.

Do you use a personal computer for business?
- ☐ Yes ☐ No

If yes, which?
- ☐ IBM/compatible
- ☐ Macintosh

Check all the ways you use computers:
- ☐ Word processing
- ☐ Accounting
- ☐ Spreadsheet
- ☐ Inventory
- ☐ Order processing
- ☐ Design/graphics
- ☐ General data base
- ☐ Customer information
- ☐ Scheduling

May we call you to follow up on your comments?
- ☐ Yes ☐ No

May we add your name to our mailing list?
- ☐ Yes ☐ No

If there is anything you think we should do to improve this product, please describe: _____
_____
_____
_____

Thank you for your patience in answering the above questions.
Just fill in your name and address here, fold (see back) and mail.

Name _____
Title _____
Company _____
Phone _____
Address _____
City/State/Zip _____

RR 114

If you have friends or associates who might appreciate receiving our catalogs, please list here. Thanks!

Name_____   Name_____

Title_____   Title_____

Company_____   Company_____

Phone_____   Phone_____

Address_____   Address_____

City/State/Zip_____   City/State/Zip_____

FOLD HERE FIRST

‖‖‖

BUSINESS REPLY MAIL

FIRST CLASS MAIL PERMIT NO. 002 MERLIN, OREGON

POSTAGE WILL BE PAID BY ADDRESSEE

PSI Research
PO BOX 1414
Merlin OR 97532-9900

FOLD HERE SECOND, THEN TAPE TOGETHER

✂
Please cut
along this
vertical line,
fold twice,
tape together
and mail.
Thanks!